Great Leaders
GROW

Also by Ken Blanchard and Mark Miller
The Secret: What Great Leaders Know and Do

Great Leaders GROW

Becoming a Leader for Life

Ken Blanchard
& Mark Miller

Berrett–Koehler Publishers, Inc.
San Francisco
a BK Business book

COLLINS BUSINESS
An Imprint of HarperCollins *Publishers*

Berrett-Koehler Publishers, Inc.
235 Montgomery Street, Suite 650
San Francisco, California 94104-2916, USA
Tel: +1 (415) 288-0260, Fax: +1 (415) 362-2512
www.bkconnection.com

Berrett-Koehler and the BK logo are registered trademarks of Berrett-Koehler
Publishers, Inc.

This edition is for sale only in India, Pakistan, Bangladesh, Sri Lanka, Nepal,
Bhutan, and Maldives, and is distributed by

HarperCollins Publishers India Ltd.
A-53, Sector 57, Noida 201301, India
Tel: +91 (0) 120 4044800
www.harpercollins.co.in

Printed and bound in India by Thomson Press India Ltd.

ISBN 978-1-60994-788-0

First Edition

16 15 14 13 12   10 9 8 7 6 5 4 3 2 1

Production Management: Michael Bass Associates

Cover Design: Irene Morris

We dedicate this book to the men and women
who inspired us to grow and helped us along the way.

Contents

Introduction

Have you ever felt like you could lead at a higher level but you weren't quite sure how to get there? Have you ever wondered how to strengthen your influence and increase your impact? Have you ever considered what enables some leaders to soar above all others? We've asked these questions and more just like them. We're convinced, after more than seventy years of combined leadership, that the path to increased influence, impact, and leadership effectiveness is paved with personal growth. There's certainly more to leadership than growth, but growth is at the heart of what creates and sustains great leaders. Growth is the leader's fountain of youth.

Growing for a leader is like oxygen to a deep sea diver: without it you die. Unlike the diver, you may not physically die—but if you stop growing, your influence will erode; and over time, you can even lose the opportunity to lead at all.

Tragically, you see these losses in organizations large and small, for profit and not for profit—leaders who attain a position of leadership and fail to keep up. Or some get a promotion based on their potential, but that potential never materializes. Or perhaps you see it in young emerging leaders who never get their shot. Their untapped potential remains untapped. What do all these situations have in common? Personal growth—or the lack of it. The failure to grow sabotages the career of more leaders than anything else.

Our capacity to grow determines our capacity to lead. It's really that simple. However, simple doesn't mean easy. Like most of life's powerful principles, the power is in the application. That's what this book is all about.

In the pages that follow, you'll go along for the ride of a lifetime with Blake, an energetic yet reluctant emerging leader. Don't get hung up on his age or lack of experience. There's some of Blake in all of us, particularly when we're faced with the challenge of growing as a leader.

Debbie Brewster plays the part of trusted mentor to Blake and shares with him four big ideas that, if applied consistently, will enable him to be a leader for life.

The idea of leading for the rest of our lives is appealing to us. We may not choose to lead in our current context or circumstances indefinitely, but name a leader you know who *wants* to become stagnant or, worse, irrelevant. We don't know any. If you decide that you want to lead well your entire life—whether in the marketplace, a nonprofit, or even in your family—you must continue to grow.

We pray that the ideas in this book will fuel your passion to grow, convince you that you can grow, show you how to grow, and empower you to grow for the rest of your life. Have fun as you GROW!

—Ken Blanchard and Mark Miller

An Unexpected Loss

"You can be a leader." The words had ricocheted through Blake's mind countless times since his father had said them. In part, because he had long had doubts about his ability to lead; also because they were the last words his father ever said to him. The next day, Jeff Brown died of a heart attack.

It had all been so unexpected, as heart attacks usually are, but in this case even more so. His dad had been in great physical shape. He'd eaten the right foods, gotten plenty of rest, and exercised three to four times per week. He and Blake had just returned from the ski trip of a lifetime. No one, especially Blake, had been prepared for Jeff's death.

A month after his father's funeral, Blake was sitting in the university library, struggling not only with his father's death but also with the idea that he could be a leader. Had his father been blinded by his love for his only son? Was this just another example of his dad's eternal optimism? Or perhaps—the scariest possibility of all—could it be true? Maybe Blake could be a leader. There were so many questions Blake wanted to ask his dad. And now, he couldn't.

"You can be a leader." Blake could still see and hear his father saying these words. When he replayed them, his responses varied from "No way" to "Really?" Blake wondered how these words would play out in the years to come. Would they be a blessing or a curse? At this point, they felt like a very heavy burden.

Jeff had been a great leader. He'd been well respected, loved by most, and very successful. He'd served his organization with high levels of integrity and skill. He had also served several nonprofit organizations in various capacities. He'd been devoted to his family and led them well. This great legacy placed a lot of pressure on Blake. Even if he could lead, he was convinced he could never lead as well as his father.

Now, Blake didn't know what to do next. He was about to graduate from college and needed a job. He was confused and scared and didn't have his father to give him advice— something he had undervalued while his father was alive. Only now did he realize how valuable that advice had been.

Hundreds of people had gathered at his father's funeral. After the service, Blake met many of Jeff's friends and coworkers. One of them was a middle-aged woman his dad had mentored for several years. Her name was Debbie Brewster; and when she introduced herself, she was fighting back tears.

Your dad made such a difference in my life, she'd said. *If there's anything I can do for you, please let me know. It would be an honor to help you in any way I can.*

Blake didn't know what else to do, so he gave her a call. She remembered him right away and sounded genuinely excited about meeting him for coffee the next day.

· · ·

"I thought I was getting here early," Debbie said with a laugh as she approached Blake, who was already anchoring a table at the back of the cafe.

He stood to greet her. "Well, Ms. Brewster, I didn't want to keep you waiting. Dad always said we honor people when we honor their time."

"He taught me the same thing," she said as she took a seat. "But please, call me Debbie." She smiled wistfully. "This reminds me of my first meeting with your father. When I called him Mr. Brown, he stopped me and said, 'Please, call me Jeff.'"

"I really appreciate your meeting with me, Debbie," said Blake tentatively.

"How can I help?" she asked.

"I'm not sure," Blake confessed.

"Okay. Let's start there." Again, Debbie smiled. "We really don't know each other," she began. "But actually, I feel like I do know you pretty well."

"Really?" Blake was surprised. "How do you know me?"

"Your father and I worked together for over ten years."

Blake wasn't connecting the dots.

"He loved you with all his heart," Debbie said.

"I know he did."

"And because he loved you so much, he talked about you all the time."

"He did?"

"Yes. We heard about your first date, your sixteenth birthday party, your game-winning touchdown at homecoming, your college search, and we even prayed for you when you had your car accident a couple of years ago."

"Wow!" Blake was visibly stunned. "Why would Dad share those things with you?"

"It wasn't just me," Debbie said.

"There are more people I don't know who know my life history?" Blake said. He didn't know if he felt flattered or a little bit ticked.

"Yes, there are several people in the company he shared with about you. It's one of the reasons he was a great leader."

"I'm confused. I thought leadership was about leadership stuff."

"Leadership stuff?" Debbie chuckled. "I guess that's a technical term."

She continued, "One of the things Jeff wanted to create was a high-performance team. He knew that the best teams always do life together. That's why we always shared about our families and other important things in our lives that were happening outside of work."

"I didn't know that," Blake admitted. "Would you mind if I take a few notes?"

"Not at all," Debbie said.

After jotting down "the best teams always do life together," Blake said, "Since you know my life history, would you mind sharing some of yours?"

"I'd be delighted," Debbie said. "First, "I don't know where my career would be had I not been mentored by your dad. But more importantly, I don't know *who* I would be. He impacted my life in profound ways."

"How?" asked Blake.

"For one thing, he taught me virtually everything I know about leadership," she said. "I *thought* I was a good leader early on, but in fact, I was a very poor leader, and my overconfidence nearly derailed my career. Then I met Jeff. At the time, he was the president of our company. I was a struggling front-line supervisor with a team that was dead last in performance in the entire company. After your father taught me what real leadership is all about, my team went from worst to first in performance. Over the months and years that followed, he continued to mentor me. I became the head of Leadership Development and eventually became head of Operations. The positive impact your father made on my life was huge."

"I've heard that from a lot of people in the last few weeks," Blake said. "Even now, even though he's gone, he's still impacting my life."

"How so?" Debbie asked.

"I'm taking notes from you on things he taught you." Blake looked up at Debbie. "That's pretty cool," he added.

"So, how can I serve you?"

"I really don't know. The last thing Dad said to me was, 'You can be a leader.' I don't know what to do with that. First, I'm not sure I believe him. Second, all I'm thinking about right now is getting a job."

"When do you graduate?"

"I graduate in three months," Blake said.

"Have you been interviewing with companies?"

"Yes."

"Any leads?"

"A few."

"What are you thinking?"

"I don't know."

"I'm getting a clear picture of your uncertainty here," she said. "What if we meet again to talk about your next steps in more detail?"

"That would be great." Blake felt relieved. He hadn't really known if his call to Debbie was the right thing to do. Now he sensed what a great ally she would be.

"Here's what you can do to prepare," said Debbie. "First, I want to understand more about your past."

"More than my sixteenth birthday party?" Blake said with a smile.

"Yes." Debbie continued, "Let's talk about your strengths, your interests, and what you've done in your life thus far that has been fulfilling."

Blake was taking notes. "Anything else?"

"Two more items: let's talk about things you're not good at, and, finally, what do you think you'd like to do for your first job—what would interest and excite you?"

"I'm not sure I can answer all those questions," Blake said while looking at his list.

"Do the best you can. It will give us a place to start."

Moving Forward

Three weeks elapsed before Blake's exams were over and Debbie had a free afternoon. The meeting was scheduled for the same coffee shop. Again, they both arrived early.

"Good afternoon!" Debbie said. "How are you?"

"I'm okay," Blake said. The truth was, he was still grieving over his father's death.

"Getting used to losing a loved one takes time," Debbie said gently. "Did you have time to think through the things we discussed at the end of our first meeting?"

"I did. Just as I feared, I don't know the answers to all the questions."

"That's okay. I rarely know all the answers to my own questions," Debbie said with a grin. "And that really doesn't diminish the power of the question. Often the search for the answer is just as valuable as the answer itself. Let's see what you've come up with so far."

They began to discuss Blake's strengths and passions. Blake was very talented, so this was a fascinating conversation.

"It's easy to see Jeff's influence on your life," she said. "After just twenty minutes, we've identified the following about you: You're comfortable meeting people. You enjoy working with children—you were a camp counselor during your high school years. You're a good student— a high GPA and other test scores helped you get into a prestigious university. You majored in business administration with a minor in marketing. And you're athletically inclined—you played several sports growing up and are still an avid skier."

Blake responded, "What does it all mean?"

"I'm not a career counselor," Debbie began, "but to me, it looks like you can do a lot of different things."

"That's what I was afraid of. What if I make a bad choice?"

"You will."

"Excuse me?" This comment really got Blake's attention.

"Sure. We all make mistakes, and we do our best to learn from them. That's one of the things leaders do extremely well."

That was the first time the "L" word had been used specifically in their conversation.

"Now that you mention leadership, Debbie, I think that's what's really got me spooked."

"What do you mean?"

"My dad and I talked about my career and my future just before he died. It was actually our last conversation."

"And what did he say?"

"He said that I could be a leader."

"And?" Debbie probed.

"I told him I didn't think so."

"Why not?"

Anytime you influence the thinking, beliefs, or development of another person, you're engaging in leadership.

"A lot of reasons, I guess. It seems like it would be hard to be a good leader. I'm only twenty-two years old; I don't know how to lead. I'm not even sure what it really means to be a leader, and—" Blake paused.

"Blake, I think you have a narrow idea about leadership. But you're not the only one. I ask people all the time if they are a leader, and hardly anyone says yes. I usually follow up that question up with 'Tell me: who has had the greatest impact on your life?' Hardly anyone ever mentions a manager or supervisor they had at work. Just like you, they talk about their father, their mother, their grandparent, a friend, or a teacher. You see, we all have the opportunity to lead in some area of our lives."

"Even me? How I am I leader?" Blake asked.

"Anytime you influence the thinking, beliefs, or development of another person, you're engaging in leadership."

"So you mean I don't have to have an impressive title to be a leader?"

"Exactly. Unless you've been living in a cave, I bet you've been influencing friends and classmates for a long time."

"I get what you're saying," said Blake, "but Dad was such a great leader." He swallowed hard. "He said he would teach me—and now he's gone." His eyes grew moist.

"I'm so sorry, Blake," Debbie said softly. "Would you like for us to reschedule this meeting?"

"No, thanks, I just need a moment."

"Let's take a break and come back in fifteen minutes. I need another cup of tea anyway."

"Thanks."

Blake walked outside and stared at the sky. It was a beautiful day. The sky was as blue as he'd ever seen, and the clouds were whiter than any he could ever remember. As the breeze blew across his face, he wiped his eyes and felt a spirit of optimism. It was as if he knew in his heart that things really were going to be okay. In that moment, he wasn't yet convinced that he could be a leader, but he was convinced he could try. He went back inside and found Debbie reviewing her notes.

She looked up. "Sure you're okay with continuing this conversation today?" she asked.

"Yeah, I'm okay. But the last few weeks have been really hard."

"I know the feeling," Debbie said. "My mom died when I was about your age."

"You didn't tell me that," Blake said in a tone of surprise.

Debbie nodded. "Although it was many years ago, it's a part of my story that is still painful. But I'm stronger today. So, I do understand some of what you're feeling. That's one reason I'd love to help you if I can. I made some mistakes—in part because of my mother's death. Perhaps I can help you avoid some of those same mistakes."

"What kind of mistakes?" Blake asked eagerly.

"I'll tell you about that later. Right now our first challenge is to help you find a job."

"That would be great. What are you thinking?" Blake had his pen in hand.

"I have a few ideas for you to consider. I think the company you work for matters. Based on the world we live in, I'm not assuming you'll be there your entire career, but a good start would be nice."

"What would a good start look like to you?" Blake asked.

"I'm thinking about a company that shares your core values. In my experience, when a person's core values are not aligned with a company's values, it's rarely a great situation—short term or long term.

"I'm also thinking about a company that has a reputation for investing in their people. These companies are harder to find today, but they're still out there.

"Finally, I believe you want a company that could provide a long-term future—just in case you want to stay."

"Wouldn't that be true at any company? I mean, if I wanted to stay and make a career, wouldn't that be an option anywhere I might work?"

"Not really. Some companies have a culture of high turnover. That's probably not where you want to start your career."

"You didn't mention leadership development." Blake added.

"You're right. I didn't for two reasons. First, I haven't heard you say you want to be an organizational leader. I heard you say that your dad believed you could lead. There's a big difference. If you don't feel like you want to be a leader, you shouldn't pursue a leadership position. You ought to be an individual contributor. That's one of the lessons I referenced earlier. When I was your age, my parents wanted me to be a teacher. They were both teachers—and teaching is certainly a noble profession. But it was not me. However, after Mom died, I decided that to honor her, I should be a teacher. Unfortunately, there were some small children that suffered through my poor career choice. Thankfully, I came to my senses after just one year in the classroom.

"You've got to pursue your dream, not someone else's dream for you. There are countless ways you can and will honor your dad. However, making a poor career choice is not one of them. If, in your heart, you can't honestly say that you want to serve people, you shouldn't pursue leadership."

"Wait a minute. You're going to have to go back to the idea of 'serving people' as a motivator for leadership."

"That's actually the most important thing your father taught me in the decade we worked together: 'Great leaders SERVE.' And it took him a long time to help me fully

understand what that means and what it looks like on
a daily basis, so I don't expect it to make sense the first
time you hear it. But make no mistake. If you don't want
to serve, you cannot be a great leader. Robert Greenleaf,
the founder of the modern servant leadership movement,
said it well: 'You have to be a servant first and a leader
second.'"

Blake was taking notes. "You said there were two reasons you didn't mention leadership development. What's
the second one?"

"Having a company that invests in leadership development is really good, but that alone won't determine
your success. If you can find a company that meets all
your criteria *and* invests in leadership development, that
would be a bonus, but it is not essential for your success
as a leader."

"What is essential?"

"You've got to be willing to GROW."

"Is that it?" Blake gave Debbie a look of disbelief.

"Yes, that's it. However, there are some specific things
you can do to accelerate and sustain your growth as a
leader."

"And what are those 'specific things'?" Again, Blake's
pen was poised.

"We can explore that together in the months to come.
For now, let's focus on getting you a job." She smiled.

They brainstormed a list of companies that might be
good candidates for Blake. Debbie gave Blake a list of
people she knew who might be able to help him. He left

with the names of several companies and people he hadn't previously contacted.

His action items were to make the contacts, try to get interviews, and be ready to share his progress at their next meeting.

"Thanks for the time!" Blake finally felt like he was making progress.

Learning to Serve

Blake contacted several companies and was able to schedule interviews with three organizations he hadn't pursued previously. He felt the interviews went well. One of the three firms offered him a job on the spot. The second sent him a letter thanking him for his interest and letting him know that the job had been filled by another candidate who more closely fitted their needs. The third invited him back for another interview.

Two out of three wasn't a bad average. His top-rated university, combined with above-average academics and social skills, made him a young man most companies would welcome to the team. He was pleased.

He asked the first company for a little more time to make a decision. The second interview turned into an invitation for a third. He wasn't sure what to make of this. Were they indecisive or just careful? Were they unsure of his candidacy? Were they probing specific concerns? He thought this would be a good conversation to have at the coffee shop with Debbie.

"How's the job search?" Debbie asked as she greeted him with a smile.

"Great!" Blake could hardly contain his enthusiasm.

"Tell me more."

"I have one firm job offer, and another company has asked me back for a third interview."

"Congratulations!" Debbie said. "I knew you could do it."

"Now I've got to make a decision," Blake said.

"What are you thinking?"

"One of the companies said they'd put me in sales."

"Selling what?"

"Hardware of some sort. I asked several questions, and they said they'd teach me all I needed to know. And the other one—" Blake began.

"The one that has invited you back for a third interview?"

"Yes. They've got several positions they think I might pursue. However, I'm a little spooked by the multiple interviews."

"Why?"

"It seems like they're pretty indecisive. You'd think they would have done this enough to make a quicker decision."

"Is that the goal?"

"What do you mean?" Blake asked.

"Is the goal of selection to make a quick decision?"

"I don't know," he said with a shrug. "I just thought time is money."

"Yes, time is money, and a poor selection decision costs both time and money. At our company, selection is considered the most important decision a leader makes. I admire a company that works diligently to get this right." Debbie paused to take a sip of tea. "What's next?" she continued.

"I guess I need to go to the third interview, and if they make me an offer, I'll make a decision."

"That sounds like a plan," Debbie affirmed. "What would you like to talk about in the balance of our time today?"

"In our last meeting, you brought up two ideas I'd like to go back to. First, you talked about what motivates leaders. Second, you said that the key to becoming a great leader is to GROW. Can we talk more about these ideas?"

"Let's talk about leadership. The fact that you want to talk about how to GROW as a leader makes me think you want to do this. But I want to be sure. In our first meeting, you were feeling the pressure to lead because your father wanted you to."

"I know," Blake said. "But I've given it a lot of thought. I realize that I don't control whether I'll be in a formal position of leadership. But I can control my readiness to lead. I'm willing to GROW as a leader in my personal life as well as take advantage of any opportunities for corporate leadership that may come my way."

"That's the best possible attitude," Debbie affirmed. "You sound like you've got your dad's optimism. If you GROW your capacity to lead, opportunities to lead usually follow. There's more to these topics than we can cover today. But we can begin the conversation.

"The motivation of a leader matters. Your dad used to ask me—and now I ask others this question—'Are you a serving leader, or a self-serving leader?'"

"Wasn't that what you were getting at during our last meeting when you were talking about being a servant first and a leader second?"

Great leaders don't think less of themselves; they just think of themselves less.

"Yes," said Debbie. "The very best leaders are others-centered. These leaders are constantly trying to help others and their organization win. In reality, when they do this, they win, too. But the very best leaders are not motivated by what they'll get in return for their actions."

"It sounds like a kind of selflessness."

"Yes, I guess you could describe it that way. Your dad used to say that great leaders don't think less of themselves; they just think of themselves less."

"That sounds hard," Blake said.

"Yes, it can be. We all have some self-serving tendencies. In fact, every morning when you get up you have a choice: to serve, or to be served. Putting your own interests ahead of those of your people and your organization is an ever-present danger that the best leaders work to avoid."

"I've never heard anyone talk about this, including my dad," Blake said.

"Most leaders don't, but your dad continually reminded me that the best leaders serve. He was a model of servant leadership."

"I don't know," said Blake, looking thoughtful. "When I hear the phrase 'servant leadership,' I can't help but think of a person who tries to please everyone, which doesn't seem very leaderlike somehow."

"You mean like a warden who lets the inmates run the prison?" Debbie asked with a laugh.

"Yeah," said Blake.

"Most people have those kinds of 'soft management' images of servant leadership," Debbie said. "That's because there are really two different aspects of leadership. The first aspect is *vision/direction*. If your people don't know where they're going, there's very little chance they'll get there. The questions the leader needs to answer are 'Where do you want us to go, and what are we trying to accomplish?'

"Once you've decided where you want to go, the second part of leadership—*implementation*—kicks in. Now the question is 'How are we going to get there?' To get where you're going, you have to serve others so they have the skills and competencies needed for the journey."

"That's interesting," said Blake. "I never thought about there being two parts of leadership."

"While it's important that the leader establishes the vision and direction, the key to a team or organization achieving that vision is having leaders who do all they can to serve their people by helping them reach their goals."

"It seems like so few organizations end up with leaders like that. More often you hear about leaders who become corrupt and fail their people. Why is that?" asked Blake.

Debbie stirred her tea thoughtfully. "If I had to guess, I'd say the two primary reasons leaders get off track are ego and fear. For many leaders, their ego is fueled by a heightened sense of confidence—you might call it over-confidence or pride. This, combined with the fear of losing control, often prevents leaders from serving people. And if there's a third and fourth reason, they would be that people aren't teaching servant leadership, and people haven't seen many positive role models."

"You said you thought my dad was a servant leader," Blake said.

"Yes, he was—the best I've ever known," Debbie agreed. "And your dad taught me that leadership is fundamentally a choice. You get to choose to engage in the behaviors I just outlined—or not. And once you've made the choice, you then get to decide how good you'll ultimately be as a leader."

"I'm guessing that's where GROW comes in," Blake speculated.

"You've got it. We'll talk about that after you get a job," Debbie smiled. "Please give me a call and let me know about your next interview."

Landing the Job

The day for the third interview arrived, and Blake was a bit more relaxed than on his previous meetings—in part because he had another job offer and in part because Debbie had defused some of his concern about the kind of organization that would conduct three interviews. As he approached the building, he had no idea what was about to happen.

He was greeted in the Dynastar lobby by Anna, his host from Human Resources. She thanked him again for investing the time in their interview process. Anna asked him about his schedule, and he shared with her that he had no other appointments that day.

"Good," Anna said. "We hope to finish our interview process today."

"Outstanding," Blake said. "Who will I be meeting today?"

"We've scheduled you to meet with several people."

Anna gave him a schedule. It looked like four new individuals, plus a lunch with a team of people, and then another meeting with one of the gentlemen he had met on his last visit.

"Any questions?" Anna asked.

"No, I'm good."

The first meeting was with a woman from Marketing. She began by introducing herself and then telling Blake about the job he was being considered for. She asked him several thought-provoking questions. Then she asked him if he had any questions. Luckily, he had prepared a short list, including a question about the company's core values and their philosophy regarding professional development. He was pleased with her answers.

The next stop was someone from Operations. After his host had asked him about a dozen questions, Blake was asked if he had any questions. Since he hadn't antici- pated meeting multiple people, he decided to ask the same ones he'd already asked in Marketing. He was pleased to get virtually the same answers.

The process repeated itself with two other indi- viduals, and then he found himself having lunch with a team of six people. They were a cross-functional group responsible for one region of the company. Each of them took about three minutes to tell his or her individ- ual story and then asked Blake to do the same. Finally, one asked Blake if he had a question for the group. At this point he decided to deviate from his prepared questions.

"Why do you like working here?" he asked.

He heard six different answers, but each sounded heartfelt.

As their time was coming to an end, one of the attendees said, "I've got just one question for you. Why do you want to work here?"

Blake answered, "When I came in the front door this morning, I wasn't sure I did. However, I've got to say that after spending the day with you, I'd like to work here because it seems like a place that is dedicated to doing the right things for the right reasons."

One of the young women in the group said, "Don't put Dynastar on a pedestal. Like any organization, we do have our issues. We're not perfect, but I think you did a nice job summarizing our intent. We hope to see you again." As the luncheon ended, Anna walked in and said, "How was your lunch?"

"It was really good. Meeting so many different people really helped me understand your company and your culture."

"You've got one more meeting before we call it a day. You'll be meeting with Alan Smith."

"Who is Mr. Smith?"

"He's our president."

"You've got to be kidding me!" Blake thought it was a prank of some sort. "Is this a test? Are you trying to see if I'll freak out? Is there a hidden camera?"

"No, it's not a prank. Relax. Alan likes to meet all of our candidates in the final stages of the process."

"Why? He's the president of a billion-dollar company," Blake said in disbelief.

"We asked him that same question a few years ago. Clearly this is a huge time commitment on his part. He told us that if we could find something more important for him to do with his time, he'd gladly do it. He believes that people decisions are the most important decisions we make."

Anna escorted Blake into Mr. Smith's office. It was very tidy and not extravagant. Shelves filled with books lined one wall from floor to ceiling.

"Good afternoon," Mr. Smith said in an energetic tone as he came out from behind his desk to greet Blake.

"It's a real pleasure to meet you, Mr. Smith."

"Please, call me Alan," he said, guiding Blake to a chair. "Why don't you sit over here and tell me about your day."

Blake recapped the highlights of his day. Even though he was uncomfortable calling the president by his first name, he told him about each of the meetings he'd attended and about the luncheon.

"Thank you for investing your day with us," Alan said. "As you can tell by now, we think people decisions are very significant. I hope you've found answers to your questions along the way."

"Yes, sir, I have. And, the answers have been amazingly consistent from all the people I've met."

"We're very thankful for the team we've assembled. They do an outstanding job. That doesn't mean we don't have problems. But we believe that solving those problems is an important way to keep getting better. Do you have any questions you'd like to ask me?"

"I see by the books you have here that you like to read. Why do you keep learning as a leader?"

"I think there are several reasons. First, I believe that my capacity to learn determines my capacity to lead. If I stop learning, I stop leading. I also believe that each of us has a stewardship opportunity to maximize the talents and gifts that have been entrusted to us. If I'm not learning and growing, it will be impossible to leverage my talents. I suppose I also believe the old saying, 'The speed of the leader is the speed of the team.' If I'm not growing, there's no way I can expect others to grow. And finally, when I'm growing, I can add more value for our people and our organization overall. There are probably other reasons—some may even be subconscious—but these are the ones that come to mind."

Blake smiled, knowing that Debbie would enjoy talking to a leader like Alan, who obviously wanted to keep growing.

> *"My capacity to learn determines my capacity to lead. If I stop learning, I stop leading."*

"All of that makes sense," said Blake.

"I've got one question for you," Alan said. "If we offer you a position on our team and promise you growing responsibility and opportunity commensurate with your ability to perform, do you think you'd be willing to make a long-term commitment to us?"

"Based on everything I've experienced during this process, yes, I will." Blake was a little bit shocked by his response, but it was from his heart. He knew this was a company that would invest in him, and he could do the same.

"Thanks again for the confidence you demonstrated in us by going through our process. Our team will evaluate your candidacy, and you'll have an answer in about a week. Thank you." Alan stood and offered Blake his hand.

"Thank you, sir. Regardless of the outcome, this has been a challenging and beneficial process. I've learned a lot about good leadership in action. Congratulations on what you and your team have accomplished here."

"As I implied earlier, we're not finished," Alan said as they walked to the door. "I believe our best days are in the future."

Blake liked the optimism Alan demonstrated.

"One more thing," said Alan. "I'm sorry about your father. He was a great leader."

"You knew my father?"

"Yes. We served on a board together many years ago. But his influence on me continues today. I guess we'll never know all the organizations he touched. But I know this—they're all better because of it." As they reached the office door, Alan said, "Perhaps this is a conversation we can continue in the future."

"I hope so," Blake said with sincerity in his voice.

As he stepped into the hallway, Anna appeared to escort him out of the building. Blake was again impressed by the coordination and professionalism he was experiencing.

"How was your meeting?" Anna asked.

"I think it went well. Does Mr. Smith really meet all the new staff candidates?"

"By the time they get this far along in the process, yes."

"That's impressive," said Blake.

"Have you had a productive day?" Anna asked.

"I think so," said Blake. "Your process has been extremely thorough. I would like to thank Dynastar for the investment in me, regardless of the outcome."

"We consider it a high compliment anytime someone is willing to entertain the idea of investing their career with us," said Anna. "Call me if you have any additional questions. Someone will be in touch with you in about a week."

As they stepped toward the door, Blake shook Anna's hand. "I hope to see you again," he said with a smile.

. . .

After the last round of interviews, Blake was eager to check in with Debbie. He contacted her office to set a meeting. It would be another two weeks before they could meet so he decided to send her a quick text.

> Debbie—thanks for your encouragement. Dynastar interview today went really well. I expect an offer in a week. B

A week later, as promised, Blake got a call from Tom with a job offer. It was on the cross-functional team he'd had lunch with. Tom said they'd love to hear his answer within a week. The start date was somewhat flexible, and the compensation was comparable to the other offer.

Blake and Debbie agreed to meet for dinner with John, Debbie's husband. Debbie had selected a very nice restaurant in the heart of downtown. Not the kind of place a college student would normally choose, so Blake hoped Debbie would offer to pay.

At dinner, John and Blake spent the first few minutes getting to know each other. Then the conversation turned to the two firms Blake was considering.

First, Debbie wanted to hear about the third round of interviews at Dynastar. Blake gave a quick summary and then told them that an offer had been extended.

"Congratulations! That is fantastic," John said. "That company has an outstanding reputation."

"So," Debbie said, "tell us about both companies and the jobs they've offered you."

Blake offered a quick summary of each one.

"Which one will you choose? Have you decided?"

"I think I'll go with the sales support position at Dynastar Industries."

"Why?"

"Several reasons. Although it was time-consuming, I did like their process, and I liked the people I met—they were very professional. Not in a stuffy kind of way— appropriately so. They seemed to have their act together.

"I think they're well led. I don't know that the other company isn't, but the influence of leadership was just much more evident at Dynastar. And I like the idea of being on a team, which wouldn't happen at the other company."

"I also felt they would be willing to make a long-term commitment to me. The president, Mr. Smith, already asked if I would be willing to make a long-term commitment to them."

"And what did you tell him?" Debbie asked.

"I told him yes. We didn't talk about what long term looks like. It may be different in my eyes. But I understood the spirit of the question. He said I'd be challenged and my responsibilities would increase based on my ability to perform. I like that."

"Sounds good to me," John chimed in.

"So, have you called him?" Debbie asked.

"No, I have until the end of the week. Have I missed anything?"

"I'm assuming you talked about salary."

"Yes, it was almost the same as the other offer. However, I feel like I'll get a lot more than a paycheck at Dynastar," Blake concluded.

"When do you start?"

"Probably a week or two after graduation."

"That's good. You and I can meet again to talk about the second issue we discussed at our last meeting before you actually start to work."

"What issue was that?" John asked.

"The issue of how to GROW as a leader," Debbie said.

"That's okay, Debbie. The position I've accepted is not a leadership role," Blake said.

"Not formally," Debbie said. "However, as we talked about earlier, leadership is not a function of title or position. I'm confident you'll have ample opportunities to lead in your new role. One last thing. From your description, Dynastar sounds like the perfect company. Just remember, there are no perfect companies. So don't be shocked when you find some flaws."

Gaining Knowledge

Blake accepted the job at Dynastar and was eager to get started. His start date was set for two weeks after graduation.

This gave him just enough time to settle into his new apartment and have one more meeting with Debbie before he began. This time, there'd be no talk of job hunting. Just one topic: how to GROW as a leader.

They met at the usual coffee shop. After brief greetings, Blake got right to the point. "Tell me how I can GROW as a leader."

"Gladly," Debbie began. "Growth is what separates living things from dying things. Organizations and people that are fully alive, GROW—leaders especially. Sometimes, people and organizations aren't really alive at all—not in the fullest sense of the word. They're not fully alive because they are not growing. Think of a heart-rate monitor. If you're not alive, the line is flat—you're clearly not growing. Growth brings energy, vitality, life, and challenge. The people I meet who aren't growing are also the ones who find life and their jobs boring. Without growth, we're just going through the motions."

"So, what I hear you saying," said Blake, "is that how well I lead will be determined by my decision to GROW or not."

"Absolutely," said Debbie. "Will you be a leader who is always ready to face the next challenge, or will you be a leader that tries to apply yesterday's solutions to today's problems? The latter will ultimately fail. The decision to GROW makes the difference. And not a short-term decision, but a decision to GROW throughout your career and throughout your life. This single decision is a game changer for leaders."

"What does growing look like in real life? I need a tangible idea of what a growing leader does."

"I think the great leaders make a choice to GROW in four areas. I'd like to talk about each one with you and then have you try them out one by one in your new job. See what happens in the real world when you do these things," Debbie suggested.

"Sounds good to me," said Blake.

"I've always been a huge fan of acronyms. Truthfully, they help me remember things. I think it may be a function of my age. So, I've been trying to think of a way to make these four big ideas fit in the acronym GROW. If you'll play along, it will help me share them with you."

"Sure," Blake said.

"The first and perhaps the most obvious is that you must decide to Gain Knowledge." Debbie wrote on a napkin:

To be a great leader, you must . . .

Gain knowledge

R

O

W

"Do you always write on napkins?" Blake asked with a smile. "They have electronic devices these days, you know."

"A leader must be ready to teach anytime and anywhere," said Debbie. "I've written on hundreds of napkins over the years. No electricity required. I can't tell you how many times people have said, 'Can I have that?' Napkins are a great leadership tool!"

"So how does a leader gain knowledge?" asked Blake.

"It begins with a commitment to become a student in several arenas," said Debbie. "Let's look at them one at a time.

"If you're going to maximize your own growth as a leader, you need to start with yourself. Think of this as gaining **self-knowledge**. You'll need a very high self-awareness. What are your strengths? What are your learning styles and preferences? What are your passions? How do you prefer to lead? What is your dominant style? Do you prefer to delegate or to coach? What is your personality type? What are the implications?

"Next, you need to gain knowledge about the **others** you want to lead—as a group and as individuals. What are their hopes and dreams? What are their fears? What can you learn about their families? Their past work experience? Their career aspirations? Their personality types? What is their individual view on recognition? Would they prefer public recognition or private? Would they be more excited about a note or a trophy? Would time off be a better reward than $100? The more you know about others, the better you can serve them.

"Next, you need to gain knowledge of your **industry**. What do you know about your industry? What has been true in the past? What is currently true about your industry that may not be true in the future? Who are your chief competitors? What are their strengths? What are their weaknesses? How has your industry changed over the last ten years?"

Blake was taking notes as Debbie continued.

"Finally, leaders need to constantly gain knowledge in the **field of leadership**. What are the trends? What are the best practices? What skills can you acquire? What skills can you sharpen? What books do you need to read?

Who can serve as your mentors? What type of continuing education makes sense? What can you do to GROW as a leader?

"All of these questions have answers. Finding those answers is contingent on the choice the leader makes—whether to focus on gaining knowledge or to remain complacent."

"This all sounds easier said than done," Blake commented. "Those are a lot of questions."

"You're right, it's not as easy as it sounds," Debbie said. "But gaining knowledge isn't difficult like curing cancer or putting men on Mars. Let me see if I can think of an example that will show you why it's so important. Aren't you a snow skier?"

"Yes."

"And I think you skied competitively?"

"I did."

"What was your event?"

"The slalom."

"Tell me if I've got this right. During competition, if you fail to make it around one of the gates, you're disqualified—is that correct?"

"Yes, it is."

"That's a perfect picture of what's happens to a lot of leaders. It's so unfortunate that many leaders fail to GROW their own knowledge and skills, because that's the first gate. If they don't make it around this first gate, they're ultimately disqualified."

"But why?" Blake asked. "Why do leaders miss something so obvious?"

"Why do downhill skiers miss a gate?"

"One of several reasons," Blake spoke slowly as he was thinking. "The most common reason is probably too much speed."

"Why would a skier have too much speed?" Debbie asked.

Many leaders fail to gain knowledge because they have too much to do—they're going too fast and trying to accomplish too much.

"Maybe he or she is pressing, trying to make up lost time. Maybe they don't know their own limitations."

"Okay," Debbie said. "Many leaders fail to gain knowledge because they have too much to do—they're going too fast and trying to accomplish too much. Maybe they don't know their own limitations. Why else would a skier miss a gate?"

"Lack of preparation. They may not have studied the course enough."

"I think the same could be said of many leaders who fail to gain knowledge. They're unwilling to take the time to GROW. Time is something many leaders convince themselves they don't have enough of, anyway. Any other reasons a skier might miss a gate?"

"Yes, I think so," Blake said. "Distractions."

"I think it's safe to say that a lot of leaders get distracted. Sometimes it's by external factors, and sometimes it's by internal factors. Distractions come in all shapes and sizes," Debbie said. "Is there some way a skier can increase the chances of making all the gates?"

"Let me think about that." Blake paused. He could remember the cold winter mornings on the mountain with his teammates and his coach. "My coach used to tell us to focus," he said.

"That's a great way to summarize what leaders must do. To consistently gain knowledge as a leader, we've got to *focus* on growing ourselves. So do you think you can use these ideas in your new role?"

"It's a lot to remember," he said.

"It is, so don't forget your slalom example. Trying to do too much and lack of focus can be disastrous. To avoid getting overwhelmed, how about you choose one thing from each of these four areas to work on first?"

"That sounds good," Blake said. "How long should I work on these things?"

"Forever," Debbie said and smiled.

"Are you kidding?"

"No, I'm not kidding. These things will always need to be on your radar as a leader, so don't worry about how long you'll need to do them. These are going to become part of who you are and what you do as a leader. Once they become part of your life, doing them won't be as hard as you think. So which one are you going to start with?"

Blake looked at the napkin and then at his notes. "Anna, the lady from Human Resources, mentioned a couple of assessments the company uses. I could talk to her and find out more. Based on what you've said, learning more about my preferences and personality would be helpful."

"That's a great start. What about gaining knowledge about the people you work with?"

"That's going to be a little tricky. I think you said a leader needs to get to know the people he or she is attempting to lead. I'm not trying to lead anyone. I'm going to be the new guy on the team—the rookie."

"I understand completely," Debbie said. "But remember, leadership is not about position. It's about influence. You should certainly be sensitive to your circumstances. But you'll still benefit greatly from knowing the people on your team. The deeper your knowledge, the more effective you'll be in the long run. As your knowledge of your people grows, so will your opportunity for real leadership—even without the title or position."

"So what should I do?" Blake asked.

"Try to learn their stories. Spend time with them individually, and ask them about their pasts, their educations, their families, their career accomplishments—anything they'll tell you. Let them decide how much of their stories they want to share. Over time, you'll learn a lot."

"I can do that."

"I know you can. Let's talk about your industry. This may be the easiest of all."

"Why would you say that?" Blake asked.

"Because you're the new guy, you can ask every member of your team, 'When you were new, what was most helpful to you as you tried to learn about our industry?'

Make a list of everything they tell you and get started working through it. You may also want to tell each person that you'll be back to see them with questions and to get more of their insight."

"I can do that, too."

"I know you can," Debbie said. "Finally, how can you begin now to GROW your knowledge and skills as a leader?"

"I'm guessing there's a lot I could do—but based on what you've said, I don't want to try to do too much."

"That's wise, because there are still other things you need to do to GROW as a leader that we haven't even talked about."

"So what would you suggest?"

"For now, let me send you a reading list of some great books on leadership. Don't feel any pressure to get through the list too quickly. Just begin the journey."

"How much do you read on leadership?" Blake asked.

"All I can. I try to always be reading at least one leadership book."

"Always?" Blake said, "What does 'always' mean?"

"I'm *always* reading about leadership. It is my chosen profession. It's how I serve people, how I add value to my organization, and how I impact the world. I know that someday I will be accountable for my leadership. Think about a doctor, or lawyer, or accountant who is trying to stay current in his or her field. If you have to visit doctors, how often do you want them to be reading about the latest breakthroughs in medicine?"

"Always." Blake smiled.

"So, reading is a great foundation for learning about leadership. Alone, it's insufficient, but it's an outstanding place to start. I'll send you some suggested titles."

"Fantastic!"

"Let's have coffee again after you've been in your new job for a week or two. I look forward to seeing how you are able to gain knowledge in the areas we discussed."

"Me, too," said Blake with a smile.

A Rocky Start

Blake was excited about his first day at Dynastar and was thankful he'd landed a job. The first item on his agenda was to meet his new supervisor. Her name was Maggie Barnwell.

Maggie was only a few years older than Blake. She was known as a hard-charger, with results as her trademark.

"Good morning," Blake said as he knocked on the door frame to Maggie's office. "I'm Blake. Today's my first day on the job. I visited with the team a few weeks ago, but you weren't there. I just wanted to stop by and say hello." With that said, he expected Maggie to invite him in. She didn't.

"Yes, I heard you were coming. Please see Ms. Grant to schedule a meeting for us this week. Ten minutes should be sufficient."

Blake wasn't sure what he'd expected, but this wasn't it. She wasn't rude—just very direct and very formal. *Ms. Grant?* He assumed this was Maggie's assistant.

As he stood there processing all of this, Maggie said, "Is there anything else?"

"No, ma'am. Well, yes, just one thing. What do I do before we meet?"

"Find Ms. Grant; tell her you need a workstation, a computer, and a partner to train you."

"Yes, I'll do that now. I look forward to our first meeting."

Again, Blake expected her to say something like, "Me, too." She didn't.

Instead, she responded, "Let's do it this week—no more than ten minutes."

Blake left Maggie's office a little stunned. He asked a man in the hallway where he might find Ms. Grant and searched out her workstation.

"Ms. Grant?" he said sheepishly as he approached her desk.

"Hi, you must be Blake."

He was so relieved. She obviously knew he was coming, and she actually looked like she was glad to see him.

"Yes, Ms. Grant, my name is Blake. Did Maggie tell you I was coming by?"

"You met Maggie?" she asked.

"Yes, I did."

"Did you call her Maggie?"

He thought about it for a moment. "No, I didn't have a chance to say her name."

"Good. 'Maggie' prefers to be addressed as Ms. Barnwell."

"Okay, thanks for telling me."

"As for me, you can certainly call me Kristie. Only Ms. Barnwell calls me Ms. Grant," she said with a smile.

Blake thought this would be a great opportunity to start learning someone's story. So he asked Kristie if there was anything else he should know about Ms. Barnwell. The next few minutes were very helpful. Blake shared with Kristie the instructions he had received from Ms. Barnwell.

"Yes, I anticipated those things. Here's your laptop. Your workstation is down the hall—number 413. I'll show you there. And your partner is Sam Caldwell. He's the best."

"Thank you, Kristie," Blake said. He realized that these few minutes with Kristie had helped mitigate his first encounter with Ms. Barnwell. His optimism was returning.

Kristie got up to show him his workstation. As they walked down the hall to meet Sam, Blake wondered if he would be more like Ms. Barnwell or Kristie. He was praying Sam would be more like Kristie.

After turning a corner, they approached an office at the end of a short hallway. At that moment, a sharply dressed man in his midthirties was coming out of the office. They almost ran into each other.

"Excuse me," the man said. "I wasn't paying attention to where I was going. I'm Sam. You must be Blake."

"Yes, sir, I am."

"No 'sirs' needed here, Blake." Sam turned to Kristie. "Kristie, is there anything else I need to know, beyond what's in his file?"

"Just one thing—he met Ms. Barnwell."

"Good. Probably should have been briefed first." Sam smiled widely as he looked at Kristie.

"Yes, but no harm done," Kristie said.

"When are you scheduled to meet with Ms. Barnwell?"

"Kristie is working on that," Blake said, "but it should be this week."

"Great. Kristie, please let us know as soon as you have that on the calendar."

"I'll be glad to. Now, I'll leave you two to get acquainted." As Kristie walked away, she looked over her shoulder and said, "Have fun!"

Sam turned to Blake and looked him in the eye. "Okay, Blake, here's the deal. We don't have a formal training program. I'm all you've got. So, I'll tell you what I think you need to know, and you've got to ask a lot of questions and take great notes."

For the next four hours, Sam talked and Blake took notes. When Sam would pause to take a breath, Blake would ask a question. Then Sam said that they needed to go meet a client who was dissatisfied with their level of service. It was one of Sam's biggest clients.

Sam briefed Blake on the way. "I'll introduce you, and I'll do the talking. Don't take it personally. It is your first day." Sam smiled.

"No problem here." Blake was relieved.

The meeting was short and direct. The client informed Sam that if Dynastar didn't step up, he'd go to a competitor. He felt he could get the same product at the same price with much better service.

Sam and Blake listened. Sam apologized for the service issues and promised to get to work on them immediately.

On the way back to the office, it was quiet in the car. The contagious smile and optimistic spirit Sam had exhibited all day had disappeared.

Finally, Blake broke the silence. "Do we have a lot of clients like that one?"

"Thankfully, not many," Sam said. "But that was one of our biggest ones."

"What's the root problem?" Blake asked.

"The industry."

"The industry?" Blake responded.

"Yes—the bar keeps being raised. Our competition is getting better and better."

"And we're not?"

"No, not really. So what used to pass as acceptable performance isn't any longer. Our past reputation is just that—in the past."

Blake remembered that one of the areas Debbie said would be important for him to learn about was the industry. So he asked Sam, "How can I learn more about the industry—specifically, our competition?"

"Great question. I'll send you some resources and a few links to check out."

It didn't feel like the path to leadership, but in his heart Blake knew that he would need to know these things and a lot more if he was going to make a difference at Dynastar.

"What's on tap for the rest of the week?" Blake asked, trying to lighten the conversation.

"Tomorrow we have a team meeting in the morning. I think you'll be with Human Resources tomorrow afternoon for orientation, and then the rest of the week we get to hang out together. We'll make some calls, go to some meetings, probably put out some fires."

"That sounds great to me. When will I meet with Ms. Barnwell?"

"Oh, I forgot. That will trump everything else. We'll check with Kristie when we get back to the office."

When they arrived back at the office, Kristie informed them that Blake's meeting with Ms. Barnwell would be immediately following the team meeting the next day.

"Okay," Sam said to Blake, "We'll meet right after your meeting with her."

"Anything I should do to prepare for the team meeting?" Blake asked.

"I don't think so. Just be ready to take a lot of notes. And, be a few minutes early."

"That sounds easy enough," Blake said with a smile.

· · ·

The next morning the meeting was scheduled to start at 9:00. Blake arrived about ten minutes early, as was his custom, and he was surprised to find everyone already there—except Ms. Barnwell.

The room was quiet. Thankfully, there was a seat open next to Sam. He sat down and whispered to Sam, "Am I late?"

"No, we're just waiting for the meeting to begin."

Sam thought this was a rather strange situation. He wanted to know more, but now didn't seem like the time to ask a lot of questions.

At 8:55, Ms. Barnwell came in.

She said, "Last month, we lost three clients. They were big clients. We can't lose any more or there will be consequences. We've also got to find clients to replace them. In the next two weeks, those sales have got to be replaced. Any questions?" She didn't really wait for an answer. There were none voiced. "We're done here."

She turned and left.

"Was that the meeting?" Blake said in disbelief. He looked at his watch—it was only 8:56!

"Welcome to the real world," Sam said with a wry smile.

"We've got to talk about this," Blake said, still stunned by what he'd just seen.

"Not now. She's going to be expecting you . . . about now," Sam said as he looked at his watch.

"Oh, yeah, I forgot. What do I say?"

"If history repeats itself, you'll not say much."

"Any advice?"

"Listen fast and take good notes."

Blake went down the hall towards Ms. Barnwell's office. He was trying to compose his thoughts. What would he say? What should he say? Should he say anything at all? With these questions racing through his mind, he arrived at her doorway still unsure about what to say.

At that moment, Kristie came out of Ms. Barnwell's office and said, "She'll see you now." At least it didn't appear by that comment that he was late.

He stepped into the office. He saw a chair in front of her desk but decided not to sit down.

"Good morning!" he said with a smile.

"Are you sure?" she responded.

"Yes, I believe so. I'm thankful to be part of this company and to be on your team."

"Listen, I know you're new, but brown-nosing won't help you one bit around here."

"If it weren't sincere, I'd agree," Blake said.

"Okay, give me one reason, besides your paycheck, that you're glad to work at Dynastar."

"Dynastar is a company with a long history of taking care of people—both customers and employees. We're known for doing the right things for the right reasons. Sorry, I think that's more than one reason." Blake tried to smile a little to test Ms Barnwell's reaction. There was none.

"Don't believe all that you hear," she said with a scowl. "And what are you smoking that would make you want to be on my team?"

"A couple of reasons come to mind. You obviously have talent, or you wouldn't have so much responsibility at such a young age. And by working on your team, I get to have Sam as my partner. I've been told he's the best there is."

"Here's my advice regarding Sam: learn all you can from him and do it quickly."

Was this her version of coaching? Was this intended to be encouragement? Or, as he feared, was this a foreshadowing regarding Sam's future? He had noted her comment in the meeting about losing clients and consequences.

"There's one more reason," Blake said tentatively. "If I may, I think I can learn a lot from you."

"Don't be too sure," she said. "Listen, I've read your file. Let's get one thing straight. The word is that you have potential. I'm not interested in potential, just performance. Performance pays the bills. Any questions?"

Blake wasn't sure if he was supposed to have any questions or not. But he did have a question.

"Just one for now," he said.

Ms. Barnwell looked perturbed.

"How can I serve you?" Blake asked.

"Serve me? You've got to be kidding," she said with a laugh. "Your challenge is to tolerate me, not to serve me."

"No, I'm serious," Blake said. "I will do everything I can to meet and exceed your expectations as I understand them. But I'd also like to serve you if I can."

"Kid, you're weird. Don't count on serving me. Just learn your job quickly and produce results. If I need you, Ms. Grant will find you. That's all."

Blake was new, but it was clear that this meeting was over. *At least Ms. Barnwell likes short meetings*, he thought with a smile as he left her office.

Out in the hall, Kristie and Sam were waiting, trying to be inconspicuous.

"How'd it go?" Kristie asked. "You were in there for a long time."

"A long time?" Blake laughed. "It was about the same length as our team meeting."

"What'd she say?" Sam asked.

"She said I'm a brown-noser."

"Did you get fired?"

"Fired? I just started."

"The last guy got fired in his first meeting with her."

"Why didn't you tell me?" Blake demanded.

"We didn't want to worry you. Besides, survival of the fittest is how things tend to work in this department. Since you've made it this far, you're probably pretty fit," Sam said.

"Why does she think you're a brown-noser?" Kristie asked.

"There may be a lot of reasons. The two at the top of the list are probably the fact that I told her I'm glad to be on her team and I asked how I could serve her."

"You did what?" Sam almost gasped when he said it.

"I asked her how I could serve her."

"What did she say?" Kristie asked, her eyes wide. "Leave out the profanities please."

"She said to perform. And that if she needed me, Kristie, no, *Ms. Grant*, would find me."

"You're lucky to still be here," Kristie said as she shook her head.

"Welcome to the world according to Ms. Barnwell," Sam said and smiled.

"I am still thankful to be here," Blake said. "It has been an interesting start—in several ways. I sense we ought to get to work."

Blake didn't know what Ms. Barnwell's issues were, but he was determined to find out. He also had a sinking feeling that if he and Sam couldn't salvage the client they'd visited yesterday, Sam might lose his job. This would be a tragedy for several reasons: Sam's family—he had three small children—would lose, the company would clearly lose, and Blake would lose. He really did want to learn from the best.

Reaching Out to Others

The meeting with Debbie couldn't have come at a better time. Blake had a lot of questions for her. They met as usual in the coffee shop near Debbie's office.

"How was your first week on the job?" Debbie asked.

"Crazy!" Blake said. "I've got so many questions."

"Let's jump in. First tell me about your team and your new supervisor."

For the next thirty minutes, Blake told Debbie about his new world. He told her everything—the good, the bad, and the ugly.

When he finished, Debbie said, "It sounds like a great place to be."

"Other than the fact that you're an eternal optimist, why would you say that? Because I've got to tell you the truth—one week in, I'm wondering if I made the right choice."

"Where there is challenge, there is opportunity. It sounds like the entire company is under competitive pressure. Your boss sounds like she's showing signs of it.

What's needed is fresh thinking and leadership. Those are two things that you can contribute. And you're lucky enough to have the best in the business as your partner. Sounds really good to me," she concluded with a huge smile.

"But how do I deal with my new supervisor?" he asked.

"I think you're off to a good start. Maybe not great, but good. She didn't fire you in the first meeting." They both laughed.

"Okay, that's true," Blake said. "But what's the deal with her, besides the pressure?"

"I don't know. But you've already established that you want to serve her. For now, all she's asked you to do is learn and produce. You can do that."

"Yes, I can. I feel like that part is going pretty well. The learning part, not the producing part. Not yet."

"Give yourself a little time. You've only been there a week."

"You'll be glad to know that I've already found ways to GROW as a leader."

"In the first week? Tell me more."

He pulled out the napkin that Debbie had written on in their last meeting.

"I can't believe you kept that," she said.

"Yes, I plan to have it framed," he said with a smile.

"You said that if I wanted to GROW as a leader I needed to start by Gaining Knowledge. Here's what I was able to do in the first week. During my orientation, I asked about the assessments that were mentioned during my interview process. The HR team arranged for me to take an assessment to help me clarify my strengths and another to understand my personality type. I think that's a huge step in knowing myself. By understanding my personality, I'll be better able to leverage my strengths and work more effectively with others."

"That's great," said Debbie.

"I've also begun to discover the stories of the people I work with. I've talked with Sam about his life and have also spoken with Kristie and two other members of the team."

"Fantastic!" Debbie said. "Just make sure you don't check the box that says 'Now I know Sam's and Kristie's story.' What you've done is tremendous—don't stop. Your goal is to go wide and deep. Your knowledge of people's stories should continue to grow over time. Every new detail is like another piece of the puzzle. The more pieces you can collect, the more you'll be able to see the true picture of who they really are. It sounds like you're off to an outstanding start. Anything else?"

"Regarding our industry, I learned in the first week that it is a changing landscape. I also learned that Dynastar is falling behind. I'm not sure what to do with that yet. But I've asked for more resources to help me understand what I might do to help."

"Let's come back to the question of what you might do to help in a few minutes," Debbie said.

"And finally, on leadership: I haven't forgotten your suggestion about reading, but I decided not to read a book right now. Instead, I contacted your company and asked for DVDs of the speeches my dad gave on leadership over the last decade. I've been going through those." His voice caught and he lowered his eyes.

Debbie knew from her own experience with the loss of her mom that he was still hurting. She didn't say anything.

Every leader is a learner.

"It's been really good," he said at last. "The more I learn about being a serving leader, the more I believe I can do it."

"You *can* do it. You've already begun the journey. Even in your first week on a new and demanding job, you've already begun to Gain Knowledge in some very important arenas. But before we move on, let me clarify something. You sounded apologetic for not reading a book in the last few weeks. You don't have to be a reader to be a leader."

"I don't? But I thought you said—"

"That's why I want to clarify," Debbie interrupted. "Reading is a very powerful way to learn—for many people. It is also the fastest way for most people to acquire information. Most of us can read much faster than we can listen. However, not every leader is a reader. But don't miss this: every leader is a learner. No matter what medium you prefer, you've got to keep gaining knowledge."

"Thanks for clarifying that. I think I'll do my fair share of reading in the future, but it does make me feel better about watching those DVDs." He smiled.

"Now it gets a little more challenging," Debbie said.

"What do you mean, more challenging?"

"Think about learning to lead like learning a martial art. As you learn and grow, each level is more challenging than the previous one. This is good; this is necessary. The increased difficulty causes you to stretch—and GROW. So, when I say the next step is a little more challenging, that's a very good thing. Remember this: growth is always the result of challenge. You grow your mind when it is challenged by new ideas or new problems or even new opportunities. Your physical strength grows when you challenge your body through exercise—when you try to lift more weight or run farther or faster. The same is true for your leadership. When you are confronted with new leadership challenges, you have the opportunity to GROW. These challenges can be self-imposed or initiated by others. It sounds like in your new job there'll be opportunities for both. Regardless, challenge is the pathway to growth."

"So what's the next challenge?" Blake was more eager than ever to GROW his leadership. Before he had a job, leadership was still in some ways an abstract idea to him. Now, he could see the realities of it in vivid detail. In just one short week, leadership had gone from a concept to something very real.

Debbie said, "To GROW as a leader, you've got to Reach Out to Others." She added the phrase to the napkin:

To be a great leader, you must . . .

Gain knowledge

Reach out to others

O

W

"Reach out to others? What does that mean, exactly?"

"It means you need to be proactive about helping others grow if you're going to grow and learn."

"How do I help others GROW?" Blake asked.

"For starters, one of the best ways to learn is to teach," Debbie replied.

"Teach what? I'm still a kid. I've only been on the job a week," Blake protested.

"I'm not suggesting that you necessarily begin teaching tomorrow. However, I don't want you to rule that out, either. The fact is, teaching is one of the primary

ways that leaders learn. I'll never forget a training program I was in where the teacher asked us to do three
things. First, he told us to take notes. He said if you don't
do that, you'll be a less effective learner. That's one of
the first things I noticed about you, Blake. You're a note
taker—which means you're an active learner."

"What else did you learn in that program?" Blake asked.

"Second, the instructor insisted that either that night
or early the next morning we review our notes and high-
light our key learnings or aha!s, and write them again in
neat handwriting."

"Why the neat handwriting?" Blake asked.

"The instructor said that most people don't look at their
notes until somebody asks them a question about what
they learned. When they refer back to them later, they
often find they can't even read their own handwriting."

"Wow, that's true with me," said Blake. "I do take a lot
of notes but often don't go back to them until much later,
when I want to look something up. Then I have a hard
time understanding my gibberish."

"Exactly. The instructor insisted that being able to
read your key learnings was paramount, because the third
thing he wanted us to do was to bring together important
people who weren't at the seminar and teach them what
we'd learned."

"Why did he want you to do that?"

"Because he knew that the best way to really learn
something is to reach out to others and teach it."

"Are you suggesting that to be a great leader I need to
be a teacher in a classroom?"

"Not necessarily. Occasionally, leaders may at some point find themselves in a **formal** teaching situation. As I think about your dad, he did teach in the classroom from time to time, and he did mentor people like me. But that was just a small percentage of his teaching. Most of his teaching was **informal**, day in and day out. He was always looking for teachable moments. And when he found them, he took advantage of them."

"Yes," said Blake. "I remember that about Dad. But he knew so much more than I do."

Debbie nodded. "He did. But it's important to realize that teaching isn't just about sharing information. It's also about helping people draw out new learnings for themselves by the questions you ask. Your question to Ms. Barnwell about how you could serve her might help her realize that she can relieve some of the pressure she's feeling by involving her people."

"So you're suggesting that I might have done a little teaching already?" asked Blake.

"I am," Debbie said.

"As a leader, your role is to teach both by sharing information as well as by asking probing questions. Every interaction with your team can offer an opportunity to teach."

"I think I get your point about asking questions, but tell me more about sharing information," said Blake.

"It's more than just sharing facts and concepts," said Debbie. "One of the best ways I've found to teach is to tell a story. Your dad was a great storyteller."

That stopped Blake in his tracks. He began remembering all the stories his dad had told him over the years and the lessons they'd contained.

"You're right," he said. "Why is that?"

"It gets past people's judgmental, critical mind—the one that wants to argue about facts and concepts. By showing your point in a story, your teaching has a chance to get through to them."

"Wow, there's more to teaching than I would have thought," said Blake.

As a leader, your role is to teach both by sharing information as well as by asking probing questions.

"It's a rich subject," Debbie agreed. "But let's go back to the issue of when to teach. Don't assume you should wait. I want to encourage you to be open to the possibilities now. Don't press; don't force it. Just be on the lookout for opportunities—formal and informal."

"Okay. I'll keep my eyes and ears open for opportunities," Blake promised.

"I can't wait to hear about them," Debbie said in her usual encouraging tone.

"I do have one more question," Blake added. "I told you about my first few encounters with my new supervisor. How does something like that happen inside a great company like Dynastar?"

"Are you asking, 'How does Human Resources miss so badly on a selection?' Don't blame them entirely. Selection is a process with a lot of variables. And besides, she apparently has some talent, or she wouldn't be in a leadership role."

"Yes, but—"

"Here's my advice for you: First, learn all you can from her—both the good things you'd like to emulate and the bad things you'll not want to repeat as a leader. Second, follow your instincts and continue to look for ways to serve her. Who knows, she may surprise you in the end."

Debbie shook her head. "I can't help but be reminded about the way I treated people early in my career. I have a scary feeling I was a little bit like your new boss."

"Really?" asked Blake. He found this hard to believe.

"Afraid so," she said. "I thought my job as a manager was to assign work, tell people what to do, and reprimand them when they didn't perform. Thanks to your dad, I grew out of that phase. I now know that leadership is about serving your people as you work together toward a shared vision."

As they prepared to leave the coffee shop, Debbie said, "Let's talk in a couple of weeks and meet again in about a month."

"Sounds great," said Blake. "I'll call your office to set the time."

"Have fun and keep growing!" Debbie said as they went their separate ways.

Teaming Up

Back at work, tensions were running high. Everyone had their own interpretations of what Ms. Barnwell meant when she'd said, "Or there will be consequences." Sam in particular was on edge.

"Sam, I've been thinking about what you said last week," Blake began.

"What did I say? I probably said a lot."

"You said our industry was changing—the service standards of the past are not cutting it today. Who's working on that?"

"On what?"

"The service standards."

"I hope manufacturing is working on it."

"Sam, I don't think hope is a strategy."

Sam chuckled. "You're right."

"Besides, service is more than a manufacturing issue. It seems like it touches several areas, including operations, sales, purchasing, and distribution. And I'm sure I'm missing somebody."

"You're right, Blake."

"I don't have a hundred-percent confidence that man-ufacturing knows the severity of the situation. They may not have talked to Ms. Barnwell." He smiled, trying to get a smile from Sam.

"You're right again," Sam said—without a smile. "What do you propose?"

"A cross-functional team to explore the issue and make recommended changes."

"And who do you think should lead the team?" Sam asked.

"You, of course!" said Blake. "You're the best. And you've got a real live case study with the gentleman we visited last week."

"That might work." It was obvious that Sam had not been thinking about a solution at that level. "But I'll tell you up front, I'm not the team leader type. What I love— and what I'm best at—is sales. Leading a team is not on my wish list."

"Can you do it this once?" Blake asked. "I'd like to be on the team with you. I think I could learn a lot about the whole business."

"Sure, I can do that," Sam added. "Honestly, because you're new, you might see some things the rest of us have missed. I'll talk to Ms. Barnwell about the idea and your involvement. Thank you, Blake."

"Thanks for what?"

"We both know my job is on the line. Thanks for try-ing to help me save it."

. . .

Sam had a very brief, as usual, meeting with Ms. Barnwell. She didn't like the idea of a cross-functional team to save existing business. She argued that it was too much like playing defense rather than offense. Sam assured her that if the team was successful, she'd be the hero. And if it failed, he'd assume full responsibility for the actions of the team. In spite of all this, she still didn't like the idea. It would be time-consuming, she said, and might cost some money. However, in light of the recent defections, she finally agreed. She wasn't excited about Blake's involvement, either, but Sam promised her that Blake was ahead of schedule, and this project would not keep him from assuming the responsibility for a region as scheduled. A real opportunity for Blake to Reach Out to Others was unfolding.

Sam assembled a powerful team. He enlisted members from the departments Blake had suggested and added a couple of others.

The team's first meeting was very productive. They attempted to pinpoint the problem and studied the data to look for clues to a solution. They finally decided that they needed more information. They needed to hear from two different groups of customers: disgruntled customers and former customers. Also, they wanted to talk to senior leaders within the company to get their perspective on the issue. Once the list was compiled, it was too long for Sam and Blake to conduct the interviews together, as they'd been planned. Blake would need to carry a full load of interviews just like the other, more seasoned members of the team. The prospect of this task excited him.

As the team was reviewing their final assignments, Blake saw a small opportunity to lead.

"Thanks for trusting me enough to let me conduct these interviews unchaperoned," Blake said. "Because I'm new, can you spend a few minutes coaching me on exactly the type of questions we'd like to have answered?" Blake knew this would help him, but perhaps more important, it would help the entire group.

Sam didn't miss a beat. "Thanks for that idea. We'll spend the next few minutes helping you create a basic group of questions. These will be the core questions we all use. Then, each of us can add our own as we see fit."

In the next few minutes, the team created three lists: one list of questions to be used with current disgruntled customers, one for former customers, and a third for senior leaders.

Blake had been given the names of one former client, one unhappy current client, and the executive vice-president of marketing.

. . .

The next day, Blake was trying to schedule a lunch meeting with one of his teammates. He thought Debbie's suggestion to know the stories of people you work with was an outstanding idea.

He stopped by to see three people, and they all declined to have lunch with him. To the third person, Sarah, he said, "Maybe next week?"

Sarah sighed. "I appreciate the offer, but I don't think next week will work out, either."

"Sarah," Blake said, "what's going on? You're the third person who has said no to lunch today, and now you say probably not for next week. What's up?"

"Listen," she said. "You're new here."

"Yes, and?"

"I think people are a little wary of the fact that you're on the cross-functional team that's going to save the planet. Pardon the sarcasm."

"Sarah, everybody's under fire, especially Sam and others with clients. You heard what Ms. Barnwell said: If we continue to lose clients, there will be consequences. Who better to lead the team to address that than Sam?"

"No one, I guess," Sarah admitted.

"I'm only on the team because Sam is the leader. You know he's my training partner."

"Yes."

"So please give me a break. I'm new, and I'm trying to learn all I can so that I can add as much value as possible. I'm going to need your help and the help of the rest of the team. Will you please work with me?"

Sarah sat in silence looking at her computer screen.

"Sarah," Blake said, "will you help me learn all that I need to contribute around here?"

"Yes—I'm sorry. You're right. We're all scared we're going to lose our jobs. I'll help you learn what you need to if you help keep us from going out of business."

"I can promise you I'll do my best. Now, will you go to lunch with me?"

"All right."

Over lunch, Blake learned more about Sarah, the team, and the business. They also agreed that before the next meeting, Blake would share with the team what he'd said to Sarah about his involvement in the newly formed cross-functional team. Sarah told Blake that she felt his explanation, combined with his sincerity, would win them over.

The team had given themselves only two weeks to get the interviews completed. This made for some very hectic and long days. But Blake was enjoying every bit of it. Just as Sarah had predicted, his explanation and passion won the team over and earned their trust. He felt he was not only growing through the process but that he was also working on something that would help the business long term.

The customer interviews were insightful. Common themes were clearly emerging. The interview with the vice-president of marketing was also telling. Marketing seemed to have no idea that the company was losing customers. Their focus was on getting new customers—not retaining existing customers. They assumed that if they got new customers, someone else would keep them.

Blake gave his findings to Sam prior to their next meeting. "Thanks, Blake. I appreciate you getting these done."

"Sam, is it okay if I do one more interview?" Blake asked.

"With who?" Sam said.

"Ms. Barnwell."

"Why? Our focus has been on senior leadership. She's not senior leadership."

"I know. But I'd like to get her perspective," Blake persisted.

"Okay, but be careful." This time it was Sam who smiled and Blake who didn't.

Blake called Kristie and asked for thirty minutes on Ms. Barnwell's calendar.

"This is highly unusual," Kristie said.

"I understand, but I'm working on this cross-functional team, and I want to be sure and get Ms. Barnwell's ideas on the subject."

"I'll ask her. When do you want to do this?"

"In the next few days if possible," Blake suggested.

"I'll follow up with you."

"Thanks, Kristie."

Blake began to think about his time with Ms. Barnwell. He really did want to learn her story. It hadn't been ten minutes since Blake talked to Kristie before she called back.

"Ms. Barnwell will see you now."

"Now?" Blake asked. "Like literally now?"

"Yes. She had a meeting canceled this afternoon. You should come now."

So much for preparation, Blake thought. "I'll come right over," he said. "Thank you, Kristie."

When he got to Ms. Barnwell's office, the door was closed. He knocked. There was no response. He waited only a moment and knocked again. Finally, he then heard her say, "Come in."

He decided to start the conversation by saying how appreciative he was that she would give him this time on virtually no notice. As he finished his sentence, he noticed that she looked different today. Granted, he'd only seen her twice before, but in both those encounters she had been hard and cold. He might have been reading it wrong but at this moment, she looked fragile.

Blake said, "Are you okay?"

The next moment of human connection totally blind-sided Blake.

"That was my mother on the phone," she said. "She has cancer."

"I'm so sorry," Blake said. "I'll leave and come back another time."

"That won't be necessary," Ms. Barnwell said with some of the old toughness returning to her voice.

"Should you go and be with her?"

"She's in Oregon."

"My question still stands," Blake said.

"I'll go see her soon." She looked away.

Was it to hide a tear? Blake couldn't be sure. He turned to leave. "I'll ask Ms. Grant to reschedule a meeting."

"Blake—" Her tone was gentler now.

"Yes?"

"Sit down and let's talk about whatever you wanted to talk about."

"Okay."

Blake began to tell Ms. Barnwell about the interviews he had conducted so far. She listened carefully and even made a few notes. She seemed totally engaged and asked several thought-provoking questions for Blake to take back to the team. Blake asked her several questions as well—he wanted to be sure he understood her perspective on the issue.

"Thank you for the time today. I'd like to be able to follow up after our next meeting." Blake wanted to be sure he left the door open for future conversations.

"That will be fine," Ms. Barnwell said. Her voice was now tired.

"Sorry about your mom," Blake said. "Hopefully the treatment will be effective."

"No. They've said her condition is not treatable. She's only got a few months left."

"I'm so sorry." Blake knew he was on thin ice but decided to speak anyway. "Listen. My dad died recently, and I didn't get to say good-bye. I really think you need to go see your mom. Who knows? She may not have months—it could be days."

Ms. Barnwell looked directly into Blake's face, and her mouth fell open. "I just realized who you are," she said. "You're Blake Brown."

"Yes, ma'am. Did I miss something?"

"Your father was Jeff Brown?"

"Yes, he was. Did you know him?"

"My first job out of college was with your father's company."

"Really? No way!"

"Yes. He fired me after a year on the job."

Blake didn't know what to say next. So he said nothing.

"I read in the paper about your father's death. But until this moment, I didn't know you were his son. You've got some big shoes to fill."

"I know. And I've decided not to fill them."

"What do you mean?"

"My father was a great man and a great leader. I guess the only mistake he ever made was firing you," Blake said with a wry smile. "I can't be my father, and I've decided I'm not going to try. However, I have dedicated myself to be the best version of me I can possibly be."

None of this was pre-rehearsed. Blake was speaking from his heart and saying things he hadn't even said to himself previously. It was an awkward moment, to say the least.

"I'll say two things about all that. 'The best version of me I can possibly be' sounds exactly like something your father would have said. And firing me was not a mistake. I'm sorry about your father—he was a good guy."

"I'm sorry about your mother. Please go see her," Blake said. "Thanks for the time today. I hope we can talk again soon."

Opening Your World

As Blake prepared for his next meeting with Debbie, he had that feeling again—that feeling that things were going to be okay. Although the circumstances looked bleak, he was optimistic. Thankfully, his group hadn't lost any more customers, Sam was still his training partner, the cross-functional team was making some progress, and he hadn't been fired yet. Maybe that was all that was fueling his buoyant spirit. Yet he felt there was something else going on—something good—but he couldn't put his finger on it.

When Debbie arrived for their next meeting at the coffee shop, Blake was already seated at a table, notebook in hand. His plate was full at work—he didn't think he could handle any more growth opportunities right now—but his curiosity was getting the best of him. He knew from the GROW acronym that there were two more ways a leader could fuel his or her growth, and he wanted to know what they were.

"How are you?" Debbie asked.

"Fantastic, I think," Blake replied.

"You think?"

"Yeah, I think things are good." Blake did his best to explain why he was optimistic.

"I'm excited for you," Debbie remarked after hearing Blake's update.

"What am I missing?" Blake asked. "Part of me thinks I should be more worried about our team."

"I'm guessing some of your satisfaction at work can be attributed to the fact that you're growing," Debbie offered.

"You're right, I am growing," Blake said.

He spent the next fifteen minutes telling Debbie about the cross-functional team and the interviews they were conducting.

"Those are outstanding opportunities to gain knowledge and reach out to others," Debbie said.

"So, what's next?" Blake asked, opening his notebook.

"First, let's review," Debbie said.

Blake smiled and pulled the napkin from his notebook.

"I thought you were going to frame that," Debbie said with a grin.

"Not until I've got the whole story."

"Okay, if you want to—" Debbie began.

Blake interrupted, reading from the napkin: "To be a great leader, you must Gain Knowledge and Reach Out to Others."

"You're off to a fast start," Debbie added.

"Thanks! It's a lot of work—especially when I'm thinking about all this in addition to my day job."

"Blake." Debbie's tone and stare were more solemn than usual.

"Yes, Debbie? What's the matter?"

"Listen, you just said something that is a huge trap for many leaders of all ages, not just new leaders starting out."

"What did I say?" Blake asked. She had his full attention.

"Please don't ever think of growing as an extra-curricular activity. Growing, for great leaders, is like breathing. It is not optional. It is *not* something you do in addition to your real job. It is at the core of your real job. Leaders—the good ones—are always learners. The way they go about it will vary from leader to leader, but it is not an option. I'm glad you've been taking good notes. I want to give you one of the most valuable thoughts I'll ever share with you as a leader."

"This sounds big," Blake said, still a bit taken aback by the passion that Debbie was exhibiting. He fumbled to get his pen in hand. "Okay, I'm ready."

"Your capacity to GROW will determine your capacity to lead. If you get too busy with your job to grow, your influence and your leadership will stagnate and ultimately evaporate."

"Thanks," Blake said sheepishly. "I was just commenting on how much is going on at work. But I really do appreciate the warning."

"I guess I should explain my passion around this. We've had several terminations recently at the office."

"And exactly how is that connected to this conversation?"

"They were all leaders."

"Why were they let go?"

If you get too busy with your job to grow, your influence and your leadership will stagnate and ultimately evaporate.

"They failed to grow with the business. I was in one of those meetings today. I guess it's just heavy on my heart. The man cried when we told him."

"How long had he been with the company?" Blake was curious.

"Fourteen years."

"Wow, that's a lot of experience."

"No, it's a lot of years. Because he wasn't learning and growing, he really just repeated his first year of service fourteen times," Debbie said. "The world is moving too fast to rely on past success and past knowledge alone. Leaders must continue to GROW."

"I've only been in my job for three months and I see that clearly," Blake said. "That's really what has gotten us in trouble. We haven't been growing in our understanding of our customers' needs and expectations. We haven't been growing in our processes and systems. I guess it's been a lack of growth by our leaders."

"Based on what you've shared with me, I think you're right. What other conclusions have you reached?" Debbie asked.

"We haven't finished our work, but based on this conversation, I think the path out of this mess is the path called growth. We've got a team meeting Monday morning. I'll keep you posted. But now I'm dying to know: what's the next way to GROW?"

Debbie said, "To continue growing as a leader, you've got to Open Your World. And you have to do this both at work and outside work. She added to the napkin:

To be a great leader, you must . . .

Gain knowledge

Reach out to others

Open Your World

W

"'Open Your World'? What does that mean?" asked Blake.

"What do you think it means?" Debbie asked.

"I'm not sure," Blake admitted.

"Give it a try," urged Debbie.

"Okay. The world's a big place. I suppose if I travel internationally, I'll have opened my world, right?" Blake said tentatively.

"That's one way to do it."

"But obviously not what you had in mind." Blake could tell Debbie had a bigger idea.

"Here's the essence of the idea: you will add much more value as a leader if you open up and expand your world with leadership experiences and life experiences."

"So what does this mean to me as a young guy in a new job, not in a position of leadership?"

"It means you need to be on the lookout for experiences inside and outside work that will make you a better leader over time."

"Help me with the 'over time' part of this." Blake still wasn't sure how this idea was connected to growing as a leader.

"Here's an analogy for you to consider. I recall your father mentioning to me that your mother is an artist."

"Yes, she paints."

"When she paints, I'm guessing she uses a palette, and on that palette, she places paint. And she does this before she actually begins painting."

"Yes, I guess so. I never thought about the sequence. We just enjoy the finished product—the painting."

"Great. That's what I'm trying to say. A leader's life is his or her palette. The experiences we have are like the colors your mom places on the palette. The more colors she places on the palette, the more she can use on the painting. It's the same for a leader."

"I got it. The more experiences we have, both in life and at work, the more colors we have at our disposal."

"Yes, you've got it. And the more colors you have, the more likely you are to create a masterpiece—in life and at work.

"And," Debbie added, "people don't see your mom working for hours, days, or weeks creating the painting—they just enjoy the finished piece. With leaders, people rarely see the behind-the-scenes activities—they just see the finished work. So that's why I suggest that if you want to grow as a leader, in addition to Gaining Knowledge and Reaching Out to Others, you also have to Open Your World."

"Okay, I'm with you conceptually. What do I do?"

"Let's start with your world **at work**," Debbie suggested. "Let's brainstorm what you could do there."

Twenty minutes later, Debbie and Blake had created the following list:

How to Open Your World at Work

- Shadow someone from another department or team.
- Work at a client's facility for a day—or longer.
- Listen in on customer calls.

- Travel with senior leaders from the company.
- Serve on a cross-functional team.
- Begin collecting best practices from top performers.
- Interview recent retirees and seek their counsel on current issues.
- Attend the grand opening of a new plant.
- Go back in the archives and watch presentations from the last decade.
- Meet with leaders from other departments to understand their issues.
- Have lunch with someone different every day until you run out of people, and then start over and do it again.
- Travel to visit your most successful locations.
- Find a mentor (formal or informal) from another department.
- Ask others who best embody the company's core values and intentionally spend time with them.
- Attend open enrollment training events that will broaden your perspective.
- Lead anything you can—project team, ad hoc group, work group, fund-raising campaign, corporate fitness effort, department meeting, corporate blood drive, continuous improvement team, or Christmas party. Chances are good you'll learn more by leading than anything else.

"Okay," Blake said. "I'm beginning to understand your comment about this getting a little more challenging. I'm assuming I need to do these things and still work to Gain Knowledge and Reach Out to Others."

"Yes, that's correct. But remember, you're in this for the long haul. You have a fifty-year career ahead of you. The things we discussed are not activities to do and check off your list. The entire idea of how to GROW as a leader is best summarized as a never-ending journey. You want to become a leader for life. Don't ever try to finish. If you ever think you're finished growing as a leader, you are finished as a leader."

"Got it," said Blake.

"And by the way, we've not even talked about how to Open Your World **outside work**. Those experiences are colors on your leadership palette as well."

"Not that I have any time right now." Blake gave Debbie a half smile as he looked at the list they'd just created. "But what type of things are you thinking about outside work?"

"Let's make a list to get your thinking started. I'll share one and you share the next. As we alternate, you can make the list in your notes."

"Okay," Blake said.

"Travel," Debbie began. "Travel is a great way to Open Your World."

This made perfect sense to Blake after he heard Debbie say it. His semester studying abroad had been a life-changing experience.

"Your turn," Debbie said.

"Volunteer work," Blake offered.

"Good. How about hobbies? Specifically, new hobbies."

"Help me with that one," Blake said as he wrote it down.

"When you take up a new hobby, what's one of the first things you do?"

With one simple question, Blake knew what Debbie was getting at. "You study and learn all you can about this new world you're entering. You grow."

"Exactly. What else?"

Again, in just a few minutes, they had created a substantial list.

How to Open Your World Outside Work

- Travel
- Volunteer work
- Hobbies
- Foreign languages
- Time with interesting people
- Read widely—beyond your industry and leadership
- Home projects—outside your comfort zone
- Mentors from fields unrelated to your own
- Exposure to the arts—museums, plays, concerts
- Campaign for a local politician
- Adventure experiences—sky diving, white-water rafting, scuba diving, mountain climbing, hot-air balloon rides, etc.

"That's an amazing list," Blake said.

"It is, but what's more amazing is the impact this type of lifestyle has on the leader. Leaders who decide to Open Their World—inside and outside work—enjoy tremendous benefits."

"I can see that, but give me a couple of the benefits as you see them," Blake said.

"When, as a leader, you consciously decide to Open Your World, you are more creative and more fulfilled. You contribute more to the organization you serve. And you are rarely bored."

"I'll keep this list handy and see how I can incorporate some of these things into my daily routine," said Blake. "Thanks for helping me with this. The kind of things you're sharing with me weren't things we talked about in school."

"I know. I'm glad to help," Debbie said. "It will be fun to see your world open up as you put these ideas into action."

A Plan of Action

The team charged with improving service was making progress—or at least they felt like they were. The interviews were complete. Everyone would agree they had learned a lot about the expectations of their customers. They had even identified some recommendations to make things better. Now they had to figure out what to do next. When the team was formed, no one really thought about next steps. The team had no authority to make changes, they could only make recommendations. And because the issues were extremely cross-functional, the solutions would be, as well. Sam called the group to order and thanked everyone for working to get the interviews done—and done in short order. He said, "Today, we need to discuss what's next with this project."

This started a lively conversation about possible next steps. The ideas ranged from the absurd to the obvious. But the longer the group talked, the further it seemed they were from consensus. Blake was quiet during all of this—listening and taking notes. He felt he'd gotten good at both during his short tenure at Dynastar.

After about ninety minutes, Sam looked at Blake and said, "What do you see that we're missing? You're the new guy; you should have a fresh perspective on this."

Blake began, "I am still new, so I may be missing something, but it looks to me like we should consider a couple of things." Blake looked around the room to see if it was safe to continue. He was pleasantly surprised—it appeared as though people were listening.

"First, should we start by summarizing our find-ings? There are at least a hundred things we learned, but they're not all equal in importance. Could we create a top five or top ten key lessons learned?"

"What would that do for us?" an older member of the team asked.

Sam stepped in. "It would give us some focus—and hopefully some traction. We probably can't, or shouldn't, attack a hundred things at once, but I like the idea of a short list. Thanks for that idea, Blake. Anything else?"

Sam's endorsement of the idea was a huge step toward credibility for Blake.

"My second thought is that we should make a few recommendations regarding each of the big issues," said Blake. "We may not know the ultimate solution, but per-haps we can offer constructive next steps." Blake thought this made sense. He remembered his dad talking about how much he appreciated leaders who offered solutions to problems.

"Blake, I think you've identified the heart of what we were charged to do. I think we were having trouble get-ting there because we were chasing a hundred things.

Thanks! So," Sam continued, "let's begin by identifying all the lessons we learned during our interviews, and then we'll start prioritizing the list. Then when it's much shorter, we'll focus on our next-step recommendations."

The balance of the meeting was extremely productive. The team didn't finish their work, but they made great strides. There was agreement on who would do what by when, and they established their next meeting date.

"Okay," said Sam, "this meeting is—"

"Sam, sorry to interrupt," said Blake. "I have one more question."

"What's that, Blake?"

"Who are we creating this presentation for?"

"That's an outstanding question," Sam said. "What do you guys think?" He looked at the team.

Everyone in the room was silent. It was as if no one had considered that question until that moment.

"Blake, who do you think this presentation is for?" Sarah asked.

"I don't know, but I think it will affect the way we present our findings and our recommendations." Virtually everyone nodded.

Sam said, "Let's add that to our action items. Everyone think about who we should present our findings to. Thanks again, Blake. That was a great catch. Meeting adjourned."

After the meeting, Sam approached Blake and said, "Man, you were huge today. You got us out of the ditch. We were floundering. Thank you!"

"I'm just glad to be able to help. I'm also thankful you've invested so much in helping me grow."

"It's part of my job."

"I disagree," Blake said politely. "You've done way more than was required. Why is that?"

"I don't know," said Sam.

"I think you do." Blake pushed just a little.

"Maybe."

"Maybe what?" Blake asked.

"Maybe I know why I do a little extra with you," Sam replied.

"And?" Blake waited.

"Two reasons I think. Trying to help you . . . helps me. I've got to be on my A game if I'm going to be able to help you."

"Trying to help you ... helps me."

"Any other reason?"

"Yeah. Someone helped me several years ago, and I've always been grateful. I guess I'm trying to pay it forward."

"Thank you, Sam! What can I do for you?"

"You're doing it. Today was so helpful. If this team is successful, maybe I can really focus on my first love—selling." Sam's gratitude was evident.

"Thanks for including me."

As Blake walked away, Sam called out to him and said, "There is one thing you can do."

"And that is?"

"Pay it forward. Someday, you'll be able to help some rookie get a great start. Invest the time—do that for me."

"You can count on it." Blake said with a huge smile. Debbie's encouragement to help others GROW was in the forefront of his thinking at that moment. "Let's meet for lunch later."

"Okay, where are you headed now?"

"To see Ms. Barnwell."

"Did she call you? If she did, I didn't hear about it."

"Nope. I'm going to get her input on who this presentation is for."

Sam shook his head in disbelief. "You're a brave man. Please don't get yourself fired."

Blake found Kristie. He told her he really needed fifteen minutes with Ms. Barnwell.

"That's a long meeting," Kristie said. "You know she likes short meetings."

Blake wished Kristie were making a joke, but he knew from his few encounters with Ms. Barnwell that she was being very serious.

"She'll ask why you want to see her," Kristie continued.

"Please tell her I have two issues. One is to seek her counsel on our cross-functional team project. The second is personal."

"Okay, I'll ask. But don't expect anything this week. No, let me rephrase that. Don't expect anything."

"Thanks, Kristie! I appreciate your willingness to help."

About an hour later Kristie called and said, "You are not going to believe this, but Ms. Barnwell will see you tomorrow at 2:00."

"I knew you'd come through for me. Thank you!"

The next day, Blake went to see Ms. Barnwell. When he entered her office, he didn't sit down. He stood and said, "Thank for giving me a few minutes today."

"Have a seat," Ms. Barnwell said.

"Ms. Grant tells me you have a personal issue you want to talk about. Are you quitting?"

"No," Blake said with a chuckle. "My personal issue is about you, not me."

"Excuse me?" Ms. Barnwell said.

"I wanted to know about your mom. I didn't mention that to Ms. Grant because I didn't know if you'd told her or not."

"Oh." Her posture changed and she hung her head. "No, I haven't told anyone. . . . Have you?" she glared at Blake.

"No. Not a soul."

"Good."

"How is your mom?"

"She's still alive."

"Have you seen her?"

"No, not yet. I'm looking for a good time."

"Forgive me for being bold, but now is the time." Blake said firmly. "Take a week of vacation and get on the plane today. What's stopping you?"

"I don't want to—" Ms. Barnwell stopped in midsentence.

"See her dying?" Blake asked, finishing her sentence.

"I'm not ready to deal with her death," Ms. Barnwell confessed.

"If I were you, I'd have a greater fear."

"What's that?"

"My greater fear would be that my mother would die without my seeing her. That kind of regret never goes away." Blake could feel the pain of the things he should have said to his father and didn't.

"Okay, I'll consider your recommendation. What else did you want today?"

"Of much less importance, I need your input on something." Blake quickly shared where the team was on their journey. "Who is our target audience for this presentation?" he asked.

"That's easy: you have two audiences," Ms. Barnwell said almost instantly.

"I'm ready."

"First, the senior leadership team—Mr. Smith and his direct reports. They can decide what they want to do with your recommendations. That's the short-term audience."

"Short-term audience? I didn't know there was a long-term audience," Blake admitted.

"I think you and your team should answer a fundamental question: 'How did we get in this situation?'"

"I think we know."

"You do?" Ms. Barnwell looked surprised.

"The team hasn't discussed it, but I think I know what we'll come up with."

"And?" Ms. Barnwell waited.

"I think we've failed to grow as leaders and as an organization," Blake said.

"That's an interesting way to think about it."

"Part of growing is listening and responding to our
customers, and being aware of changes in our industry.
We haven't done either very well."

"That's very helpful and affirming."

"Affirming?" Blake said.

"Yes, it confirms my hunch regarding the long-term
audience. Your findings—specifically how we got into this
mess—need to be shared with *all* our leaders. You've got
to teach them about the mind-set that allowed us to get
out of touch and the practices necessary to prevent this
from happening in the future."

"It does sound like a teachable moment," said Blake.
"Thanks for your thoughts. He stood to leave. "Is there
anything I can do for you today?"

"Just what I said in our first meeting—tolerate me and
produce results." She smiled a tired smile.

"Please go see you mother. Go today."

Blake turned and walked out. He realized he'd just
gotten the last word with Ms. Barnwell. He had the feeling it was something that happened very rarely. He hoped
it meant she was listening.

Walking toward Wisdom

Debbie and Blake had agreed to meet in the coffee shop but Blake asked if they could meet later than usual. Debbie had no problem with that.

This time, Debbie arrived first. Blake came rushing in, still five minutes early, but feeling as if he were late.

Before he even said hello, Blake said, "Sorry, I'm late." He was almost out of breath.

"Good evening, Blake," Debbie said. "You're not late."

"I knew it was going to be close. I had a meeting this evening."

"That's a little unusual," Debbie said. "Why'd you guys meet so late?"

"Oh, it wasn't a meeting at work. I decided to look for a way to apply a few of your GROW concepts outside work."

"Good for you! What'd you come up with?" Debbie asked with a smile.

"As you know," he began, "I've been fairly busy. But I didn't want to use that as an excuse. Instead, I started reviewing my notes, looking for a way to multitask."

"You were looking for a way to multitask regarding your leadership development?"

"Yes, I wanted to Reach Out to Others in a way that fits with who I am and what I'm passionate about. Do you remember when we talked about my strengths and passions?"

"Yes, I do."

"One of the things I've always enjoyed is working with kids."

"Yes, I remember, you were a camp counselor during your summer breaks in high school."

"See if you can connect the dots. I love kids. One of the ways leaders grow is through cross-cultural experiences. Plus, leaders grow as they help others grow. What do you get when you combine all of this?" Blake asked.

"I'm dying to know," said Debbie.

"I signed up to tutor a child from Asia. We're working on English as a second language."

"That's awesome! I'm proud of you. I'm guessing this is going to help you more than you know."

"Maybe it will, maybe not. But that's not my motivation. I was really looking for a way to help someone else. Sam has really helped me at work, and he challenged me to pay it forward in the future—to help someone else get a great start. I decided I didn't have to wait until later. Although I know I'll enjoy some personal benefits, I'm really doing it for Deshi—that's my new friend's name."

"Was tonight your first meeting with Deshi?"

"Yes."

"How was it?"

"Challenging. He really doesn't speak any English. I think all I managed to communicate tonight was 'My name is Blake.'" He laughed.

"No, you did something else far more important. You communicated that you care. I can't wait to see how this goes in the weeks and months to come. I want to hear about all the lessons you learn on this adventure." Debbie took a sip of her tea. "So what's going on at work?"

Blake spent the next fifteen minutes updating Debbie.

"It looks like you are finding opportunities to help others GROW. I see several teaching opportunities—both formal and informal."

"You are correct." There was no doubt in Blake's mind that he was growing as a leader. "In the time we have left," he said, "I really want to know the fourth arena in which leaders need to GROW."

"Napkin, please," Debbie said.

Blake opened his notebook and pulled out the artifact of the previous meetings.

"You know what this has become?" Blake asked.

"What?"

"It's more like a treasure map than a napkin."

"I like the spirit of that metaphor," Debbie said, "but there is a fundamental difference."

"And that is?"

"In a treasure map the prize is at the end."

Blake picked up from there. "And this treasure can be found all along the journey."

"Exactly. Growth for the leader is the treasure that funds the future journey. Stop finding the treasure along the way and the journey ends. That's why what I'm teaching you applies to leaders at every phase of their careers."

They were now both looking at the ideas Debbie had shared previously. "There's at least one more way in which the best leaders GROW," she said. "As they journey, they Walk toward Wisdom." Again, she wrote on the napkin.

To be a great leader, you must . . .

Gain knowledge

Reach out to others

Open your world

Walk toward wisdom

"That sounds deep and almost presumptuous." Blake said. "Can I—or any leader—actually influence our growth in wisdom?"

"Absolutely," said Debbie.

"Please tell me more." Blake felt this was the most daunting of the four ideas he and Debbie had discussed.

"What are your questions? What are your reservations about this?"

Wisdom is the application of knowledge, discernment, insight, experience, and judgment to make good decisions when the answer may not be obvious.

"It seems like wisdom is something that's only given to special people, like saints and sages. Although I suppose if you gain knowledge, reach out to others, and open your world, you will get wiser. Does it happen automatically?"

"Wisdom can be an outcome of gaining knowledge, reaching out to others, and opening your world. However, it is *not* automatic. How do you define wisdom, Blake?"

"I don't know. I'll have to think about that a minute." They sat quietly for a moment while Blake gathered his thoughts.

"Okay, here goes. Wisdom is the ability to apply your knowledge, skills, and life lessons in the appropriate ways at the appropriate time."

"That's a pretty good definition. Wisdom is different from knowledge. It's deeper than mere knowledge. It's the application of knowledge, discernment, insight, experience, and judgment to make good decisions when the answer may not be obvious. The ability to do that is not automatic. There's an ancient proverb that challenges us to *pursue* wisdom. That's what the best leaders do."

"So how do you pursue wisdom?" Blake asked.

"Growth in wisdom has no formula, but it almost always involves at least one of four elements: rigorous self-evaluation, honest feedback, counsel from others, and time."

"It sounds like you've given this some thought," said Blake.

"Very much so," said Debbie. "Let's take a quick look at each element."

"**Self-evaluation** is the ability to look in the mirror and tell yourself the truth. Not your version of the truth—the real truth. What are you doing well? Where are you struggling? What are your real strengths? What are your weaknesses? What are you doing that's adding the most value? What are you doing that adds the least value? It was Socrates who said, 'The unexamined life is not worth living.' Self-evaluation is a tremendous starting point as we pursue wisdom."

When Debbie paused, Blake said, "That sounds like it could be hard."

"It is one of the hardest things a leader must do. And to compound the situation, the higher you go in an organization, the harder it is to do an honest self-assessment."

"Why is that?" Blake asked.

"There are probably many reasons, but two immediately come to mind. Successful leaders often fall prey to their own press clippings. If the enterprise they lead is successful, they can overvalue their contribution to that success. That leads to pride and ego and other destructive attitudes that impede honest self-evaluation. The second reason is that leaders are often removed from the real, day-to-day work. It is not their work. As a result, they can become isolated. Isolation impedes honest self-evaluation."

"That reminds me of a story I heard recently about a man who owned a hotel chain," said Blake. "He was hearing complaints about the service in his hotels. He commented that he personally had never had a bad experience in one of his hotels. Clearly, he was out of touch. Is that the kind of thing you're talking about?"

"Exactly," said Debbie.

"So how does a leader maintain perspective and do an honest, rigorous self-evaluation?" Blake asked.

"Here are a couple of ideas: Ask yourself the questions we just discussed on a regular basis. Become a heat-seeking missile regarding the truth. And, don't *ever* rely completely on self-evaluation. It can yield tremendous results, and it can also fail you."

"So, that's where the next idea comes in, right?"

"You're correct. In addition to self-evaluation, those pursuing wisdom need **honest feedback**. And as we've just established, that can sometimes be hard to get. But it is usually available. There are a lot of ways to get the type of feedback we're talking about. For some leaders, their organization helps them."

"How?" Blake asked.

"In some companies, feedback is part of the culture. It can come from your supervisor, your peers, and even those you lead. How does Dynastar help leaders get feedback?"

"I don't know. But I can ask Sam." Blake made a note to himself. "What if Dynastar doesn't help with this?"

"It doesn't matter. You've got to get feedback anyway. Ask people you work with what you should *start doing, keep doing,* and *stop doing.* You can do this in the form of an e-mail or a face-to-face meeting. You can probably learn a lot by just asking those simple questions."

"Sounds easy enough."

"It is simple, but it may not be easy. It amazes me how many people will not tell you the whole truth. That's why getting feedback from others is tremendously helpful, but usually not enough on the path to wisdom."

"Luckily for me, I can play the new card," Blake said.

"What's the new card?"

"I can approach people and legitimately say, 'I need your help,' which I do. 'I'm new around here, and I really do want to get off to a good start. Can you please give me some feedback? I have only three questions. What should I start doing that I'm not currently doing? What should I stop doing? What should I continue to do?' I think the new card will help."

"You may be right. If I were you, I'd play that card as long as I could. But in addition to rigorous self-evaluation and feedback, you need to seek **counsel from others**," Debbie said.

"What's the difference between counsel and feedback?"

"Great question! Generally, feedback is about the past, and counsel is about the future. Counsel is often derived from the experience of the person you're talking with. You get to benefit from their experiences and possibly even their wisdom. Both feedback and counsel are extremely helpful for leaders."

"Okay, so what type of counsel about the future am I looking for?"

"I'm talking about your pursuit of wisdom, on *any topic*. Be sure to proactively seek the counsel of others."

"How does that work?" Blake felt like he was trying to catch up on this one.

"Again, there is no formula, but a tremendous skill you can cultivate is the ability to ask outstanding questions."

Blake asked, "Can you give me a few examples?"

"Sure. Here are a few of my favorite generic questions," she said.

- What decisions in your life have made the greatest contributions to your success?
- What are the biggest lessons you've learned so far in your career?
- What do you know now that you wish you had known 20, 30, 40 years ago?
- What books have had the greatest impact on your life and your leadership?
- If you were my personal coach, what advice would you have for me?

As Debbie shared each question, Blake captured it in his notes.

"This is a lot to take in," he said.

"I don't ask all these questions in every situation. And with some people you'll be pursuing a specific point of view on a specific topic. Questions are a great way to glean wisdom from others."

"I like that idea," said Blake.

"Gleaning wisdom from others can save you a lot of grief. It means you don't have to make all the mistakes yourself. That realization alone is a little bit of wisdom."

"Tell me about the fourth element of wisdom," said Blake.

"The fourth element is **time**," Debbie said. "Wisdom is accumulated over months, years, and decades. You've got to stay with it. The pursuit of wisdom, like the other areas of growth, is never-ending. Don't try to rush it— and never stop seeking it. If you'll do the things we've discussed, over time, you will grow in wisdom."

"Wow! Prior to this conversation, wisdom was off my radar. Now, I know it has to be part of my growth agenda—even if I am only twenty-two."

"The earlier you start, the more time you have to gain wisdom," said Debbie. "And trust me, time flies. If you're not careful, you can end up like the man my company had to let go of recently. Lots of years, not much wisdom."

"I'm sure I'll have a lot of challenges and my fair share of problems during my career, but this won't be one of them," said Blake. "I will work diligently to grow in wisdom."

The Presentation

The team was getting closer to its first presentation. Blake shared with them Ms. Barnwell's ideas about the short-term audience and the long-term audience. The team liked the concept. As they made their final preparations, they were trying to decide who would actually do the presentation. After an hour of pros and cons, the team decided to have three presenters. Sam would set the context, Blake would present the "state of the industry," and the senior marketing person on the team would present the team's recommendations.

Blake was honored to have been given the chance to present to the short-term audience: the senior leadership. He certainly didn't want to overplay it in his own mind, but in some way, it felt like he would be teaching. As Blake thought about this, he knew it would be a tremendous opportunity to GROW.

The team decided to present Ms. Barnwell's idea of addressing the long-term audience—all the company's leaders—as one of the recommendations. They would wait and see how the senior leaders would respond. The presentation was scheduled for a Tuesday morning. The team had been given one hour to present, and they allocated another hour for questions.

As the team and the senior leaders were gathering for the meeting, Blake noticed that Ms. Barnwell was not there.

"Sam, did you invite Ms. Barnwell?" Blake whispered.

"Yes, but Kristie said she was on vacation. Couldn't change it. I pressed a little and Kristie said to let it go. And then I got the strangest text message this morning."

"From Ms. Barnwell?" Blake asked.

"Yes, I think," said Sam. "What do you mean, you *think*? Was it from her or not?"

"Here's the deal. First, the message was *so* out of character—"

"What did it say?"

"It said, 'Thank you for helping save our company. Good luck today!'"

"That is amazing." Blake was pleasantly surprised.

"But wait, there's more," said Sam.

"More?"

"Yes, this is the part that makes me really wonder if it was from her."

"I'm waiting."

"It was signed 'Maggie.'"

"You're kidding!"

"No. For real—take a look." Sam showed Blake the text.

"That's cool," Blake said. "Ms. Barnwell—Maggie— was instrumental in the work this team has done. Maybe we can find a way to leverage her wisdom more going forward."

"We'll wait and see. As strange as this may sound, I wish she were here today and not on a beach somewhere."

Blake held his tongue before commenting. He wanted to honor the confidence Maggie had bestowed on him. He hoped she was with her mom and not on the beach. He said, "Sam, I'm going to interpret her absence as confidence in us."

"I love your optimism." Sam smiled. "Let's do a presentation."

The meeting went as planned. From the courteous and spirited tone of the question-and-answer session, the senior leaders were impressed with all three presenters. Although Sam's team had several recommendations, they did not directly point to the leadership shortcomings that let the company get in this bind. Alan Smith, the company president, called them on this.

"Ladies and gentlemen, thanks for your presentation today. It was well conceived and well presented. And I'm particularly intrigued by your recommendation that we share some of this presentation with a broader group of leaders. What I didn't hear is this: what is the key message we want the other leaders to understand?"

The team was silent. They were not prepared for this question.

Sam spoke for the team. "We've not completed our work on that, but we can get back to you in the next few days with a communications plan."

Alan wasn't satisfied. "What's the root problem here?" He voice was a little more forceful. He looked at Blake. "Blake? What do you think?"

Blake took a deep breath and thought, *If Maggie didn't fire me, maybe Alan won't, either.*

Blake answered, "We've not helped our leaders or our organization grow sufficiently to meet the changing demands of our world. We got caught providing yesterday's answers to today's problems."

The team members sat in shocked silence. Most of them had never been in a meeting with Mr. Smith. It was anyone's guess how he would handle the unvarnished truth.

"Thank you, Blake. I think you're right," Alan responded. "Sam, we need that communications plan you referenced. The end of the week will be sufficient. I'll take the action item to figure out how to prevent this from ever happening again. This meeting is adjourned." It was only then that the team let out a collective breath.

Before everyone could even get out of their chairs, Alan said, "Blake I'd like to see you in my office."

Blake's team members looked horrified. Was Blake going to be drawn and quartered?

"Yes, sir," Blake said.

Heading for the door with the rest of the team, Sam passed Blake and whispered, "I'll pray."

Blake only managed a tiny smile.

Two minutes later, Blake was in Mr. Smith's office. He decided to let him speak first.

"I just wanted to thank you again, Blake. I've heard about how you contributed to the success of this team—heck, they tell me it was your idea to start with. So, thanks for all of that. But, more importantly, thanks for telling the truth today. Truthtellers are desperately needed around here. You showed courage, too. That's another fine and essential attribute for a leader."

"Thank you, sir. Dad always told me that truth is a leader's best friend."

"He's right, and that friend sometimes brings pain. Today was painful for me. This has happened on my watch. It's going to take some time to work through the implications. One conclusion that is immediately apparent is that being a leader dedicated to lifelong learning and personal growth is not the same as creating a culture of growth. I've always been committed to growing as a leader, but I've failed to create an organization that shares my passion for growth. I've got a lot of work to do." He looked out the window and asked, "Does that match your conclusion on this issue?"

"I think there is wisdom in what you said, sir. We all have a lot of work to do."

"I don't know if it's wisdom or not, but it is the truth. We *do* have a lot of work to do."

"Please let me know how I can serve going forward."

"I don't know the specifics, but I'm going to put together a group to help me think about this. I'm going to count on you being a part of that group."

"It would be my pleasure, sir. Thank you."

"No, Blake, thank you."

. . .

Blake returned to Sam's office feeling elated, but he kept a straight face as he lowered himself into the chair in front of Sam's desk.

Sam looked up with concern. "Do you still work here?" he asked.

"Not only do I still work here, but I've even been thanked for my truthtelling."

"You're kidding," said Sam.

"I kid you not. Plus, I've been asked to serve on a group to ignite a culture of growth at Dynastar. The place we're going to start is to help the leaders in this organization GROW."

Sam's eyebrows shot up. "That sounds like a challenging assignment. Do you have any ideas about that?"

Blake smiled. "I do," he said. "Let me show you a few." He pulled out his notebook and showed Sam the notes from his meetings with Debbie:

To be a great leader, you must . . .

Gain Knowledge
- Yourself
- Others
- Industry
- Leadership

Reach Out to Others
- Formally
- Informally

Open Your World
- At work
- Outside work

Walk toward Wisdom
- Self-evaluation
- Feedback
- Counsel
- Time

Sam took a moment to study Blake's notes. "This looks interesting," he said. "Can you teach me what it all means?"

"I'll be happy to," said Blake.

Room to Grow

As usual, Blake reached the coffee shop early. Still, he was not early enough to arrive first. But this time it was Ms. Barnwell, not Debbie, he'd arranged to meet. His boss sat waiting for him at a table by the window.

"Good afternoon, Ms. Barnwell."

She welcomed him with a smile. "From now on, it's Maggie, okay?"

"Yes, ma'am," he said as he took a seat across the table from her.

"Not 'ma'am.' Just 'Maggie.'"

Blake nodded. This was the first time he'd seen her since she'd returned from her vacation. He couldn't put his finger on it, but something in her appearance had changed dramatically. Her face bore the signs of grief, but it also looked more open and less guarded.

"I heard your presentation went splendidly, Blake," she said.

"Thanks greatly to you, Ms. Barn—I mean, Maggie. Your ideas about the short-term and long-term audience for our recommendations really resonated."

"From what I hear, you made quite an impact at that meeting," she said. "I know your father would be proud of you."

A pang went through Blake, and he lowered his eyes. The triumph of his meeting with the president was a moment he would have loved to have shared with his dad, but he knew he never could. When he looked up again, Maggie was staring at him.

"The reason I asked you to meet me here is because I personally wanted to thank you for pushing me to go see my mother," she said. "I arrived two days before she died."

"How did it go?" asked Blake.

"I was able to tell her I loved her, something I hadn't said in years. Frankly, it was something I hadn't *felt* in years. But there was genuine love between us during those last two days. We talked about our regrets and resentments, and as soon as we did, they seemed to disappear. By the time Mom slipped into her coma, she looked so peaceful—" Maggie bit her lip and gazed into her coffee.

Blake wondered if his boss was even ready to come back to work. It looked as though she were still struggling with her loss.

"I'm so glad you got to say good-bye," Blake said. "That's something I didn't get to do, since my dad's death was so sudden."

"But your dad knew you loved him," she said. "Even when I worked for him, you were the apple of his eye. And this path you're on—this determination you have to grow as a leader—is the best way you can honor him."

"I hope so," said Blake. "And I'm excited about the steps we're taking to get Dynastar back on track. A lot needs to be done, and I think I can really be of service."

"No doubt you can," said Maggie. She frowned and some of the old toughness came back into her face. "But you've still got a lot to learn. I had a chance to look over those reports you turned in last week. You got the territories mixed up, and it appears you're not yet clear on the concept of gross sales versus net income. I want you to get those reports right. Oh, and could you start producing some sales results?"

Blake smiled wide. This was the Ms. Barnwell he remembered.

"Yes, I can do that," he said. "I know I have a long way to GROW."

Resources to GROW

We hope you enjoyed Blake's story.
In the following pages, you'll find resources to help
you GROW along your own leadership journey.

Personal Assessment

Rate each statement using the following scale:

5 = Completely Agree; **4** = Partially Agree; **3** = Neither Agree nor Disagree; **2** = Partially Disagree; **1** = Completely Disagree

	Your Score
Gain Knowledge	
I know my own strengths and weaknesses.	_____
I know the people I lead on a deep level (personally and professionally).	_____
I know my industry extremely well.	_____
I have a high level of mastery of the principles and practices of leadership.	_____
I have a detailed, written personal development plan.	_____
Total	_____

Reach Out to Others	
I am always looking for ways to invest in the growth of others.	_____
I have ongoing mentoring relationships with emerging leaders.	_____
I frequently see and seize teachable moments.	_____
I frequently share what I'm learning with others.	_____
I have developed a high level of mastery communicating my point of view on leadership.	_____
Total	_____

Open Your World

I constantly look for opportunities to grow
at work.   _____

I constantly seek new experiences outside
the workplace.   _____

I have a mentor(s) who helps me grow.   _____

I am always looking for additional
opportunities to lead.   _____

I see every day as an opportunity to
learn and grow.   _____

Total _____

Walk toward Wisdom

I consistently tell myself the truth regarding
my leadership.   _____

I actively seek feedback from those I know
to be truthtellers.   _____

I have a group of people I trust to give me
counsel on important issues.   _____

I have mastered the art and discipline of
asking profound questions.   _____

I am fully committed to a lifelong pursuit
of wisdom.   _____

Total _____

What's Next?

In case you were wondering, there is no value in the assessment you just completed—the value lies in what you do next. Here are a few suggestions for you to consider.

Look at the four sections of the assessment. How can you do more in the area in which you scored the highest?

Next, look at the area in which you are the least proficient today. Pick one item—just one—and create a plan. For example, if you realized that in the Walk toward Wisdom section you don't have a group of people you can trust to give you counsel on important issues, you can start today forming a personal board of directors. Or, if you had a low score on frequently sharing what you're learning with others, think of someone you can meet with to share what you've learned in this book.

After you've successfully done one thing, choose another. When you've done them all, start over and do them again. Don't stop. The point is to stay on the journey.

If there were a bonus question, we can think of one that is worth more than the twenty you just read. It is this:

Do you want to be a leader for life?

That is the question that really matters. If you remember only one thing from this book, we hope that it is this:

Your capacity to GROW determines your capacity to lead!

Other Assessments

Many assessment tools are available to help you better understand your personality, strengths, weaknesses, and preferences. Here are a few you may want to explore.

DISC Profile

This powerful tool can help you significantly improve your work effectiveness. With its unique Self-Assessment and unlimited 360° Observer Assessment, the DISC Profile is designed to give you a comprehensive view of how you interact with others in everyday situations. The goal is to understand your personal chemistry in order to enhance your relationships. Once you know the characteristics of your behavioral style, it is easy to see what drives those around you and how you can interact more successfully with them. For more information, visit www.kenblanchard.com.

Myers-Briggs Type Indicator

The Myers-Briggs Type Indicator® is another instrument used by many organizations, large and small. Results of this assessment provide a framework for understanding individual differences in the workplace. When you understand your type, you can tailor your work to your style and find the best approaches to decision making, developing skills, communicating, and coping with change. For more information, visit www.myersbriggs.org.

Gallop Strengths Finder

Gallop's online assessments, introduced in *Now, Discover Your Strengths* and *StrengthFinder 2.0,* have helped millions of people discover their top talents. For more information, visit www.strengthsfinder.com.

Blanchard Certified

Blanchard Certified offers an online program to understanding self—your temperament, your needs and values, and your communication style—including information on how to use this knowledge to be more effective as a leader. For information, visit: www.blanchardcertified.com.

The SERVE Model

As Debbie pointed out in the story, the best leaders serve others. Servant leaders are those whose goals are focused on the greater good. In *The Secret: What Great Leaders Know and Do*, Ken Blanchard and Mark Miller give an in-depth description of the ways in which great leaders SERVE. It's an acronym that represents the following leader behaviors:

See the Future

Envision and communicate a compelling picture of the future. Leadership always begins with a picture of a preferred future.

Engage and Develop Others

Recruit and select the right people for the right job while creating an environment where people wholeheartedly invest themselves in achieving the vision.

Reinvent Continuously

Possess a never-ending focus on improvement. Progress is impossible without change.

Value Results and Relationships

Generate positive, measurable results, and cultivate great relationships with those you lead. Ultimate success always includes both people and performance.

Embody the Values

Live in a fashion consistent with your stated values. People learn more from what a leader does than from what a leader says.

Recommended Reading

One of the questions we get a lot is, "If you were going to recommend a good book, what would it be?" This is a difficult question, one that usually prompts a follow-up question: "What topic are you interested in?" As we begin to narrow the conversation, we can often make an informed recommendation of books that have helped us on our journey.

Two factors affect whether or not a book is right for you: content and timing. A book may not speak to you today based on your circumstances—and it may prove extremely valuable at some point in your future. With that disclaimer, we've put together a small sampling of the many books that have helped us at some point during our lives. We hope that some of these books may serve you as well.

Awaken the Giant Within by Anthony Robbins
Barbarians to Bureaucrats by Lawrence M. Miller
Built to Last by Jim Collins
Communicating for a Change by Andy Stanley and
    Lane Jones
The Contrarian's Guide to Leadership by Steven Sample
Courageous Leadership by Bill Hybels
The Effective Executive by Peter Drucker
The Five Dysfunctions of a Team by Patrick Lencioni
Good to Great by Jim Collins
In Search of Excellence by Tom Peters
Integrity by Henry Cloud
Jump Start Your Brain by Doug Hall
Leadership and the New Science by Margaret Wheatley

The Life You've Always Wanted by John Ortberg
Margin by Richard Swenson
Necessary Endings by Henry Cloud
The Power of Full Engagement by Jim Loehr and
    Tony Schwartz
The Power of Positive Thinking by Norman Vincent Peale
Resonate by Nancy Duarte
Teaching to Change Lives by Howard Hendricks
Use Both Sides of Your Brain by Tony Buzan
Wooden on Leadership by John Wooden and Steve Jamison

Acknowledgments

This is tough to write. There are hundreds, probably thousands, of men and women who have helped us GROW. To name them individually would be impossible. Yet the type of growth we're advocating is never a solo endeavor.

Our journey to grow began at home with parents who encouraged us to give our best—whatever we were doing. They wanted us to be all we could be. Then there were the teachers—at all levels—who did more than teach us the facts; they fueled our curiosity and challenged us to GROW. Then there were the managers and leaders who shaped us early in our careers—they were our exemplars for the necessity of learning. So are the mentors in our lives who continue to instruct and challenge us—too many to list by name!

We also must mention that The Ken Blanchard Companies and Chick-fil-A get it. Both of our companies have made the strategic bet that if people grow, the business will grow. That belief, combined with leadership that walks the talk, has contributed immensely to our individual growth.

Next, our families. Both of us have been blessed with wives who inspire us to keep learning and growing. We also have children who have joined us on the journey of lifelong learning. This is one of our greatest blessings.

There are a few people we do need to single out by name. Margery Allen and Renee Broadwell provided support behind the scenes that helped make this book possible. Finally, Martha Lawrence has given a gift to everyone who will read this book— her insights and immense talent made this a much better book!

To all of you who continue to encourage, inspire, and assist us as we GROW: Thank you!

About the Authors

KEN BLANCHARD

Few people have impacted the day-to-day management of people and companies more than Ken Blanchard. A prominent, gregarious, sought-after author, speaker, and business consultant, Dr. Blanchard is universally characterized by his friends, colleagues, and clients as one of the most insightful, powerful, and compassionate people in the business world today.

From his phenomenal best-selling book, *The One Minute Manager* (coauthored with Spencer Johnson)—which has sold more than thirteen million copies and remains on best-seller lists—to the library of books coauthored with outstanding practitioners—*Raving Fans, Gung Ho!, Leadership and the One Minute Manager, Whale Done!,* and many others—Ken's impact as a writer is extraordinary and far-reaching.

Ken is the chief spiritual officer of The Ken Blanchard Companies, an international management training and consulting firm that he and his wife, Dr. Marjorie Blanchard, founded in 1979 in San Diego, California. He is also a visiting lecturer at his alma mater, Cornell University, where he is a trustee emeritus of the board of trustees. Ken is the cofounder of The Center for *FaithWalk* Leadership, which is dedicated to challenging and equipping people to Lead Like Jesus.

Ken and Margie, his wife of forty-nine years, live in San Diego. Their son Scott Blanchard, his wife Madeleine Blanchard, and their daughter Debbie Blanchard hold key positions in The Ken Blanchard Companies.

MARK MILLER

Mark Miller began his Chick-fil-A career working as an hourly team member in 1977. In 1978, Mark joined the corporate staff working in the warehouse and mailroom. Since that time, he has provided leadership for Corporate Communications, Field Operations, and Quality and Customer Satisfaction, and today he serves as the Vice President, Training and Development. During his time with Chick-fil-A, annual sales have grown to almost $4 billion. The company now has over 1,500 restaurants in 38 states and the District of Columbia.

When not working to sell more chicken, Mark is actively encouraging and equipping leaders around the world. He has taught for numerous international organizations over the years. His topics include leadership, creativity, team building, and more.

Mark teamed up with Ken Blanchard to write *The Secret! What Great Leaders Know and Do.* More than 350,000 copies of *The Secret* are in print, and it has been translated into more than 20 languages. His latest book, *The Secret of Teams*, was released in 2011.

Mark enjoys an active lifestyle. As a photographer, he enjoys shooting in some of the world's hardest-to-reach places, among them Mount Kilimanjaro, Everest Base Camp, and the jungles of Rwanda. He's also a runner, recently completing his first marathon.

Mark and his wife, Donna, have two sons and have been married for almost thirty years.

Find Mark online at www.GreatLeadersServe.org and on Twitter @leadersserve.

Services Available

The Ken Blanchard Companies® is a global leader in workplace learning, productivity, performance, and leadership effectiveness that is best known for its Situational Leadership® II program—the most widely taught leadership model in the world. Because of its ability to help people excel as self-leaders and as leaders of others, SLII® is embraced by Fortune 500 companies as well as small to midsize businesses, governments, and educational and nonprofit organizations.

Blanchard® programs, which are based on the evidence that people are the key to accomplishing strategic objectives and driving business results, develop excellence in leadership, teams, customer loyalty, change management, and performance improvement. The company's continual research points to best practices for workplace improvement, while its world-class trainers and coaches drive organizational and behavioral change at all levels and help people make the shift from learning to doing.

Leadership experts from The Ken Blanchard Companies are available for workshops, consulting, as well as keynote addresses on organizational development, workplace performance, and business trends.

Tools for Change

Visit kenblanchard.com and click on "Tools for Change" to learn about Workshops, Coaching Services, and Leadership Programs that help your organization create lasting behavior changes that have a measurable impact.

Global Headquarters

The Ken Blanchard Companies
125 State Place
Escondido, CA 92029
www.kenblanchard.com
1.800.728.6000 from the U.S.
+1.760.489.5005 from anywhere

Join Us Online

Visit Blanchard on YouTube

Watch thought leaders from The Ken Blanchard Companies in action. Link and subscribe to Ken Blanchard's channel, and you'll receive updates as new videos are posted.

Join the Blanchard Fan Club on Facebook

Be part of our inner circle and link to Ken Blanchard at Facebook. Meet other fans of Ken and his books. Access videos, photos, and get invited to special events.

Join Conversations with Ken Blanchard

Ken Blanchard's blog, HowWeLead.org, was created to inspire positive change. It is a public service site devoted to leadership topics that connect us all. This site is nonpartisan and secular, and it does not solicit or accept donations. It is a social network, where you will meet people who care deeply about responsible leadership. And it's a place where Ken would like to hear your opinion.

Ken's Twitter Updates

Receive timely messages and thoughts from Ken. Find out the events he's attending and what's on his mind @kenblanchard.

Mark's Twitter Updates

Receive timely messages and thoughts from Mark. Find out the events he's attending and what's on his mind @leadersserve.

Stay in Touch

We'd love to hear about your journey and learn from your success. You can contact Mark Miller at GreatLeadersSERVE.org. On this site he'll share ideas and best practices from leaders around the world. We invite you to join the conversation!

Ken Blanchard and Mark Miller

The Secret
What Great Leaders Know and Do, Second Edition

The first edition of *The Secret* introduced a profound yet seemingly contradictory concept: to lead is to serve. Join struggling young executive Debbie Brewster as she explores this secret to truly motivating and inspiring people. Along the way, she learns why great leaders seem preoccupied with the future; why and how people on "the team" are invariably key ingredients of success or failure; what three arenas require continuous improvement; why true success in leadership has two essential components; how to knowingly strengthen—or unwittingly destroy—leadership credibility; and more. This second edition includes a section summarizing *The Secret*'s key points, making it even easier to use this book as a learning and development tool.

Hardcover, 144 pages, ISBN 978-1-60509-268-3
PDF ebook, ISBN 978-1-60509-470-0

BK® Berrett–Koehler Publishers, Inc.
San Francisco, *www.bkconnection.com*

800.929.2929

Also by Mark Miller

The Secret of Teams
What Great Teams Know and Do

Teams are critical to the success of every organization. But what separates the teams that really deliver from the ones that simply spin their wheels? Mark Miller uses a compelling business fable to reveal critical insights that can dramatically transform any organization. Debbie Brewster has been promoted and is now struggling with taking her new team to the next level. On her journey she learns from three very different teams—the Special Forces, NASCAR, and a local restaurant. Debbie and her team discover the three elements that all high-performing teams have in common, how to change entrenched ways of thinking and acting, what you have to do to optimize each of the three elements of a successful team, how to measure your progress, and more.

Hardcover, 144 pages, ISBN 978-1-60994-093-5
PDF ebook, ISBN 978-1-60994-109-3

BK® Berrett–Koehler Publishers, Inc.
San Francisco, *www.bkconnection.com*

800.929.2929

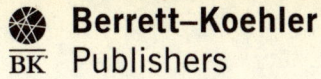

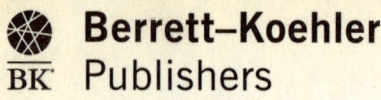
Berrett–Koehler
Publishers

A community dedicated to creating
a world that works for all

Visit Our Website: www.bkconnection.com

Read book excerpts, see author videos and Internet movies, read
our authors' blogs, join discussion groups, download book apps, find
out about the BK Affiliate Network, browse subject-area libraries of
books, get special discounts, and more!

Subscribe to Our Free E-Newsletter, the *BK Communiqué*

Be the first to hear about new publications, special discount offers,
exclusive articles, news about bestsellers, and more! Get on the list
for our free e-newsletter by going to www.bkconnection.com.

Get Quantity Discounts

Berrett-Koehler books are available at quantity discounts for orders
of ten or more copies. Please call us toll-free at (800) 929-2929 or
email us at bkp.orders@aidcvt.com.

Join the BK Community

BKcommunity.com is a virtual meeting place where people from
around the world can engage with kindred spirits to create a world
that works for all. BKcommunity.com members may create their own
profiles, blog, start and participate in forums and discussion groups,
post photos and videos, answer surveys, announce and register for
upcoming events, and chat with others online in real time. Please join
the conversation!

Certified

Corporation
bcorporation.net